THE AEGEAN

A SEA-GUIDE TO ITS COASTS

AND ISLANDS

THE AEGEAN

A Sea-Guide to its
Coasts and Islands

H. M. DENHAM

JOHN MURRAY

Contents

Illustrations

Sketch maps and line drawings in text by Elizabeth Scott

* *Photographs by the author.*

Photographs by Greek photographers supplied by courtesy of the Greek National Tourist Organisation.

Acknowledgements

I am grateful to George Millar who first encouraged me to write on the Aegean; to Robert Somerset and to Lord Merthyr who provided me with additional information on certain ports; and to Jehane West whose knowledge of present Greek conditions, as well as its ancient history, has helped me considerably. I would also like to thank my wife who went through my typescript and made good some of my deficiencies.

'The grand object of travelling,' wrote Dr Johnson, 'is to see the shores of the Mediterranean.—On these shores were the four great empires of the world—the Assyrian, the Persian, the Greek and the Roman. All our religion, almost all our arts, almost all that sets us above savages has come to us from the shores of the Mediterranean.'

Preface

This book is designed to help those who wish to sail in the Aegean. It is the result of various cruises, both in steam and under sail, as well as periods of camping, mountain scrambles, shooting and shore excursions.

During these years I have kept a record of local conditions, sailing craft, ports and anchorages, the latter having been recently collated for fellow members of the Royal Cruising Club.

Although I always had a latent enthusiasm for sail, my interest in the Aegean began the hard way. At the age of 17, when a midshipman in a battleship at the Dardanelles during the First World War, my action station was normally in the crow's nest, a waist-high canvas structure mounted on the head of our topmast. When the bugle for action sounded, I had to struggle up a swaying Jacob's ladder to reach my lofty perch; armed with a telescope and part of a chart, I then waited for the guns to go off. My duty was to report where our shells had fallen, and any signs of enemy activity.

It was in the intervals when our guns were silent that the Aegean landscape gradually grew on me. History seemed to spread itself out on a gigantic map around me; from my crow's nest on the Hellespont I could see the Plain of

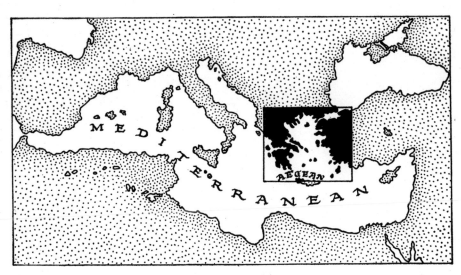

Troy to the southward, Gallipoli (often too close) to the north, the islands of Tenedos and Imbros and, sometimes, the tall rounded summit of the Samothrace. In the vicinity were one or two of the alleged tombs of Homeric heroes and other historic landmarks, all of which, with the aid of my scrap of chart, could be identified.

Some months later I was sent to command the Navy's smallest patrol-boat on a Macedonian lake where we guarded the frontier between the Allies and Bulgarians. Here was the ideal life, often riding round the country to win over the goodwill of the village mayors, shooting duck, stalking boar, fishing for perch, excavating Roman baths with a fanatical archaeologist and living in an isolated lake encampment. This pleasant interlude ended all too quickly and I soon found myself once more at sea in various small craft examining the coast for U-boats and thus gaining a more intimate knowledge of the Aegean.

During the years between the Wars, when I was serving with the Mediterranean Fleet, a proportion of our time was spent in the Aegean. There were many opportunities for rough shooting in the winter, for scrambling over mountains and exploring under sail in ships' boats many of the small coves and sheltered anchorages which I was subsequently able to visit again some years later.

Twelve years ago, when I was able to cruise in my own yacht, I became captivated by the Aegean—not only for the beauty of the country and the liveliness of the small ports, but for their association with the past. Many places have Hellenic and medieval remains and here the link with ancient history is evident and vivid. Even without these remains, it needs only a little research in museums, libraries or early writings to link all that you see today with the great events that once took place there. Thus, by recreating the past, what had perhaps appeared to be an uninspiring anchorage becomes once more alive.

To clarify descriptions of some of the more remote places considered suitable for yachts, a number of sketches and rough harbour plans are provided. With few exceptions these are not published elsewhere, the data having been obtained from early surveys corrected for recent physical changes and based on my own soundings.

I must make it clear that none of this information is meant to take the place of official publications, *Sailing Directions* or charts. It is intended only to augment them to help those coming to the Aegean by sea: to choose where to go and how to get there; what to do and how to go about it after they have arrived.

H.M.D.

Introduction

GENERAL INFORMATION

Spelling of Greek Names. During recent centuries, names used for islands and ports were very often those given by the Venetians, e.g. the island of Telos was called Episcopi; Piraeus, Porto Leone; Chios, Scio; etc.

British charts used either:

(a) the British conception of the phonetic spelling of Greek names, e.g. Euboea, for Συβοια, or

(b) a transliteration of the sound of the Greek name, e.g. Evvia, or

(c) a mixture of the two, Evvoia, or

(d) The Italian name, e.g. Stampalia for Astypalia.

Some of the Italian names on the British charts are not now recognizable to the Greeks. If, for example, you enquire of a Greek for the harbour called St Nikolo in Kithera, he will not understand; the Greeks know this port only as Avlemona. Similarly, Cape Matapan to the Greeks is always Tenaron and Navarino is Pylos.

There are also the recently eliminated Turkish names such as the widely-known yacht harbours of Tourkolimano and Passalimani, which only a year ago reverted officially to their old names of Munychia and Zea respectively.

The Turkish Government has acted in a similar way and new Turkish names have now been given to places known for centuries under their Greek or Venetian names.

Throughout this book I have observed the following system:

Such well-known places as Athens, Rhodes, Crete, Salonika, I have written according to our English custom, but to make sure that every place may be easily found in the Index I have in most cases inserted its alternative name. For the less well-known places I have used the spelling of the modern Greek chart.

The Hydrographer of the Royal Greek Navy is engaged in compiling a chart giving an accepted spelling of all charted places.

Port Officials are not mentioned at each place since at every small Greek port there are normally both a Customs Office and a Port Authority. In very small places the local policeman sometimes acts on their behalf. The harbour officials dress like the Navy, though they are not sailors, nor are they administered by the Admiralty. On a yacht's arrival a 'sailor' from this office will usually direct the yacht to a berth, and he will then ask for Ship's Papers. The complication of having both Customs and Port Authority papers has very recently been overcome by the issue of what might be termed a ship's passport (called a Transit Log by the Greek authorities)—a novelty quite unknown in other countries. This is issued at the 'Port of Entry'* on the yacht's arrival from her last foreign port.

No harbour dues are imposed on a yacht.

Fuel and Water being an important concern for a small cruising yacht, the Greek authorities have now issued a list of 'Supply Ports' where these commodities can be obtained. At some of these places water and fuel have always been obtainable, but they have now been provided with a diesel fuel pump on a section of the quay marked by blue and yellow zebra stripes; this pump also supplies the fishing craft. At major ports diesel fuel may be obtained without tax.

Petrol must be bought from a local filling-station or store, in one's own containers. According to the locality in Greece, petrol may be sold either by the gallon, the litre or the kilo, and is usually about the same price as in England.

It is not always advisable to fill the drinking water tanks of a yacht from the hydrant on the quay. Local people sometimes have good reason for buying their water from a spring in the country and, though more expensive to hire a water-cart, it is to the advantage of a yacht also to do so. When visiting Turkey, unless one is sure of the quality of the fresh water, it is advisable to wait and replenish on return to Greece. As far as possible observations on the quality of the fresh water have been made at each port listed.

Food and Drink. As the enjoyment of cruising in Greece can be so easily marred by stomach troubles, a few notes on the local food and drink are necessary. Very few English digestions are immune to Greek cooking, which is often very greasy with strong Greek olive oil added to almost everything.

In all the small restaurants it is quite in order for the customer to enter the kitchen and choose his dish from the wide copper pans spread out on the charcoal stove—generally there are chicken, lamb stew, stuffed tomatoes, savoury rice, and fish soup etc., all looking most inviting, as well as the Greek dishes such as *Dolmades* (meat and rice in vine leaves), *Moussaka* (a sort of shepherds'

---

* Most of the larger ports and one or two small ones are Ports of Entry and are notified as such under the sub-heading of 'Port Officials' at those places concerned.

pie with cheese on top) and *Pasticche* (baked macaroni with meat and cheese). These should be avoided in the evening as they were probably cooked for the mid-day meal and have been re-heated. Usually there is a charcoal grill, and lamb cutlets or fish cooked on this is a safe bet; but be sure to say 'without oil' ('ohee Ládhi') when ordering or you will find cold olive oil has been poured over your grill. Fish is almost invariably good and fresh. Nearly all restaurants have little dishes of *Yoghourt*, and also delicious *Baklava* (honey-cakes with almonds). Never order your whole meal at one time, or you will find that the dishes will be brought all together, and by the time you have eaten your first course the second will be congealed.

In early spring the following are usually available:

Fish

Tsipoúra		French Dorade
Sinagríthi		Sea Bream
Varvoúnia		Mullet
Maríthes		Whitebait
Octopóthi		Octopus
Calamári		Squid
Astokós	late	Lobster
Garídes	spring	Prawns

Meat

Arnáki	Lamb	—usually good
Hirinó	Pork	
Brizóles	Chops	
Bon Filet	Steak (fillet)	
Móskari	Veal	
Nefró	Kidneys—usually good	

Butter is unobtainable except in Athens, Corfu and certain towns much frequented by tourists.

Fruit and Vegetables—Early in the season are:

Oranges, cherries, loquats, beans and peas, and courgettes.

Some of these begin to go out of season in May and are followed by tomatoes, cucumbers, aubergines, lettuces, peaches, apricots and figs. Later there are grapes and melons.

Anything eaten raw should be washed with a few grains of permaganate of potash.

Wines

Kampá, both red and white in bottles, is obtainable at ports near Athens.

Etálya, a dry white wine, is quite pleasant and can be bought on draught.

Doméstica, a dry white, can be bought in bottles at many places.

Retsína can be bought everywhere. All right if you can enjoy resinated wine.

Local Vermouth and Three Star Brandy are passable aperitifs: *Ouzo* (a form of Raki) is the local spirit and is obtainable everywhere on draught.

'Fix' beer, obtainable nearly everywhere, is excellent.

Accents have been indicated to help prospective shoppers

Health. The incidence of typhoid and tetanus varies from year to year in Greece, but there is always some, and it is sensible to be inoculated. Practically all the well-known medicines and drugs can be bought in Athens and possibly in the few big towns, but nowhere else, so it is advisable to have a well-stocked medicine chest. The *Yachting World* diary gives an excellent and comprehensive list which covers most eventualities. Two useful additions are phtalysulphathia-zole* and entero-vioform, as, inoculated or not, many people in the Medi-terranean become afflicted with some form of colic, particularly if eating ashore.

Malaria appears to be completely stamped out.

Nowadays in Greece there is no trouble in finding a doctor on the larger islands and even in the smaller places there is generally a qualified medical practitioner, a chemist and, at the worst, probably a midwife. *Sailing Directions* mention when a hospital is to be found at the larger ports. In Turkey medical facilities outside the large towns fall short of the Greek standard.

As good health largely depends upon the purity of drinking water, it is recommended to take the opportunity if possible, of filling a yacht's tanks, where recommended in this book.

Shooting. Shooting cruises in Greece, usually in British yachts, continued until nearly the beginning of the First World War. Large schooners sailed from England in January or February, collected the owner and guests in Italy or Malta and then mostly proceeded to the Albanian coast and North Greece. There they found an abundance of duck, partridge, quail and woodcock. Those who entered the Aegean were limited to red-legged partridges,† hares and rabbits on the Islands, wild goat at Anti-Milos, and duck shooting on the Vardar marshes near Salonika. With the exception of the wild goat, all these still exist.

On the Anatolian coast of Turkey a number of British and French residents from Istanbul and Smyrna used at one time to take advantage of the good shooting.

Fishing. Because the rivers of Greece are largely mountain torrents, dry in summer, shore fishing is confined to the lakes and certain estuaries. Though fly-fishing in Macedonia was mentioned by a contemporary of the Emperor Hadrian, it has not, so far as is known, been practised since. In some of the lagoons they take mullet and turtles; on parts of the Anatolian coast the Turks have established trapping devices, with canneries close by.

* Trade name 'Sulphathalidine'.

† Being non-migratory they are always to be found on most islands; woodcock, snipe, quail, geese and duck only come in spring and autumn.

On the Macedonian lakes a number of primitive boats are used for laying out nets; on Lake Beshik there were recently as many as seventy of these craft. Both here and on other lakes perch and carp are fished.

At sea a variety of fish is caught, almost entirely at night, by groups of 'mother-ship and five ducklings' with nets, using gas-lamps. French dorade, sea bream, mullet, whitebait, sardines and prawns are among those caught by this means; octopus, squid and lobster are caught by spearing and in pots. There are many schools of dolphin in Aegean waters; small sharks are sometimes seen, though only rarely have they been known to attack people. The tunny also pass through the Aegean, though they are rarely hunted. The waters off the Anatolian coast, which receive the flow from a number of small rivers, yield the most fish, and are frequently poached by the Greek fishermen. This encroachment by the Greeks is always the excuse offered by the Turkish Customs guards for having been too trigger-happy on the innocent approach of a strange yacht.

By far the best fishing is in the Bosporus. Here it is seasonal. At Istanbul the bulk of Turkey's sea produce is sold, consisting chiefly of anchovy, mackerel, sardine, turbot and tunny.

PILOTAGE

Calm as a slumbering babe
Tremendous Ocean lies
ODYSSEY V.256

The vagaries of the winds prevent the Aegean being classed as an ideal sailing ground; yet the appeal of the small sheltered ports and anchorages together with scenery of bold and striking contrasts more than compensate, and make the Aegean the most attractive part of the Mediterranean.

The winds described on page xix though largely predictable may also come up suddenly and without warning; but as the Aegean Sea is relatively small and well spaced with islands shelter is reasonably close at hand.

The coast, both of the mainland and the islands, is mostly hilly or mountainous, and with the exception of the islands lying a long way from the mainland and of part of Anatolia, the country is green and often wooded. The entertaining small ports, full of local colour, are often tucked round secluded corners, and reveal themselves quite unexpectedly.

When making an extensive cruise it is prudent to make use of the prevailing north wind and plan accordingly: i.e. during the Variables of May and June, it is recommended to make as far north as possible, and then, with the beginning of the Meltemi in early July, start cruising southwards with a fresh to strong fair wind behind one.

Though the *Mediterranean Pilot*, Vol. IV (*Sailing Directions*) states 'The navigation of this storm-ridden archipelago at night presents many difficulties . . .' this warning need not be taken too seriously in the summer months when currents and tidal streams are slight, and when during the dark hours there is usually a flat calm. This is when sailing yachts normally prefer to anchor.

This book cannot hope to cover all existing anchorages in the Aegean; nevertheless it gives a good representative selection of them. Naturally any attempts to write accurately on pilotage without careful comparison with existing information would be futile.

In the last century a number of British yachts, large vessels by today's standards, visited the Aegean. The owners often published accounts of their cruises and even the guide books provided information for yachtsmen—giving details of ports and anchorages as well as advice on chartering local boats. The accounts of these early cruises are of limited value, since the yachts, being large and without auxiliary power, used to visit only the larger bays and anchorages which are of little interest for a yacht today.

The most valuable information both on pilotage and archaeological matter is to be gleaned from reports by Her Majesty's surveying vessels and from observations by early travellers.

Some of the smaller plans of minor Greek ports are no longer printed on the charts because this information is now considered to be redundant.* Nevertheless, it is remarkable how valuable and accurate they are, and how little changed these coasts would be but for the following occurrences:

(1) **Removal of Ruins.** Looking back on the many places visited in Greece and Turkey in the last few years, it is surprising how much the man-made features have changed since many of the early British surveys were made. At that time most of the ancient sites were much more extensive than they are today, especially in the more remote places, where buildings and masonry have largely vanished, in a few places completely: thus certain landmarks are now no more.

---

* Recently the Hydrographer of the Royal Greek Navy has made surveys of a number of small ports and anchorages; these are now published in Greece. Many of them are helpful to yachts cruising in Greek waters. Similar plans now published by the British Admiralty are becoming available through Admiralty chart agents. The Turkish Admiralty has also established a hydrographic office, but surveys are still awaited.

(2) **Changes in the Sea Bed.** In certain areas the seabed also has changed in character and depth; occasionally a conspicuous above-water rock has toppled over, or a pot-hole has appeared where one intended to anchor.

When details of seamarks, depths, lights etc. require some elucidation, or are at variance with information furnished in official publications, I have endeavoured to explain them in this book.

Entering the Aegean. The Western approaches, the Eastern Gateway and the Dardanelles passage are described in this book. The other means of entering —via the Corinth Canal, a route used by many yachts—is also mentioned, but the extensive approach to the Canal via the Ionian Islands, the Gulfs of Patras and Corinth is outside its scope. This route is both interesting and practical, clearance into Greece being obtained either at Corfu, Argostoli or Patras.

The Weather and its Implications. Few countries as small in area as Greece afford such a variation in climate. In some years, at the end of March you may find summer at Kalamata (Southern Peloponnesus) and sea-bathing at Rhodes— at the same time it may be winter in Arcady and on the lakes of Macedonia.

However, throughout the Aegean, the latter part of April, May and June are undoubtedly the best and most settled months for cruising. By June the temperature has begun to rise sharply, and though since the last century we no longer take elaborate measures to protect ourselves from the hot sun, it is nevertheless oppressive in July and August.

Winds. The early Greeks associated the eight winds with certain seasonal conditions, and this phenomenon may best be summarized by the symbols carved on the octagonal marble Tower of the Winds standing intact below the Acropolis at Athens. It once had a water clock and a sundial. Its eight sides still face the important points of the compass, each being portrayed by a carved figure symbolic of the eight winds:

N.
Boreas
or the
Tramontana
the violent piercing north wind: a bearded old man well wrapped and booted, holding high the hood of his cloak.

N.E.
Kaika
now called
Grego
the north-east wind, so cold on the Attic coast. The olives falling from the old man's charger depict the unfriendly nature of this wind to the vital Athenian fruit crop.

E. Wind

E.

Apeliotes   the more kindly east wind is portrayed by a handsome youth carrying the
now called   various species of fruit favoured by this wind.
Levante

S.E.

Euros   the frequently stormy south-east wind represented by an old man.
the present
Souroko

S.

Notos   the south wind—an unhappy clouded head, implying heat and damp. The fact
now the   that the figure is emptying a water-jar implies that the wind brings heavy
Ostra   showers and sultry weather.

S.W.

Libs   the south-west wind so unfavourable to vessels leaving Athens. A strong
now called   severe-looking man is pushing before him the prow of a ship.
Garbis

W.

Zephyros   the soft and kindly west wind, represented by a lightly-clad youth carrying
now called   flowers and blossom, and gliding along contentedly.
Ponente

N.W.

Schiron   the dry north-west wind: a robust bearded little man, wrapped and booted,
now called   pouring water from a vase to denote the occasional rain from that quarter.
Maistro

During the last few centuries evidence from ships' narratives reveals that the
Greek pilots had almost no logical understanding of changes in weather. Their
predictions were invariably dictated by certain changes in shrubs, plants and
other omens, e.g. certain pilots believed that the first appearance of the egg-
plant was followed by a north-easter of some continuance. If at sea when
confronted with foul winds they would always seek shelter, having too great
a deference for the elements to think of contending against them.

Not only do seafaring Greeks use the Italian names for some of their winds, nowadays they also box the compass in Italian; this is a legacy from the Venetians.

The Prevailing Summer Wind, so often referred to in this book, is the Meltemi ('Etesian' wind in British *Sailing Directions*). According to Herodotus it begins with the 'Rising of the Dog Star' and continues until the end of the summer. It may be expected to begin, therefore, in early July and to continue sometimes until the middle of September. Caused by the low-pressure area over Cyprus and the Middle East, this wind has a mean direction between N.W. and north, except in the Turkish Gulfs, Kithera Channels and towards Rhodes where it blows almost west. It may be expected to start each day towards noon, reaching a velocity of force 5 to 6 and sometimes 7 by afternoon, and falling off towards evening. Quite often, without warning, it blows all night without diminishing in strength. When these conditions obtain the wind on the Anatolian coast suddenly veers to N.N.E. during the hours of darkness. The Meltemi blows with the greatest strength from the middle of the Aegean towards the south. In the extreme north this wind is light, and in some northern areas a light sea-breeze is drawn in from the south.

The tall islands, which might be expected to form a lee for a sailing yacht working to windward, do not help, for the wind is always more violent under the mountainous coast than it is a few miles off. Certain islands, Andros for example, develop a heavy cloud formation over the mountains, an indication of strong north winds.

Summer Anchorages, July to early September, are therefore on the southern or south-eastern side of the islands, and though often open to the south, there is small risk during these months of the wind suddenly shifting in that direction. Vessels with power, wishing to work northwards, often start at night or early morning when the sea has gone down, and continue their passage until the Meltemi begins to impede their progress the following afternoon.

Other Seasons. In May and June there are usually light variable winds; also after the Meltemi season in the latter part of September and early October, when there are often pleasant sailing breezes. After the Autumn months, gales from N.E. may be expected and in December, January and February from south and S.E. Though many of the caiques take their chance of putting to sea most of the winter months, it is not until April that reasonable weather for sailing begins to set in.

Tides and Seiches. Admiralty predictions indicate a maximum rise of a few inches at some places to $2\frac{1}{2}$ feet at others. The level of the water is far more influenced by wind and seasonal conditions than by tide and, therefore, for practical purposes tide need not be considered.

It is necessary to watch the sea level during a strong wind of long duration, and to bear in mind that in certain gulfs in the Northern Aegean the sea level during winter months may drop at least $2\frac{1}{2}$ feet and remain at this level for many weeks.

In places where violent squalls sweep down from the mountains miniature 'tidal waves' or Seiches may be formed; the surge from this is apt to sweep round the quay and call for some attention to a yacht's stern warps.

Currents. There is a general trend of current from north to south; in light settled weather it is very slight, but with strong sustained northerly winds it may start running with a maximum velocity up to 5 or 6 knots in certain channels—especially Doro and Kea, and between Andros and Tinos.

Only in the rare event of a strong southerly wind in the Autumn is this current likely to be reversed.

There is a gentle north-going stream setting up the southern part of the Turkish Anatolian coast. This meets the general southgoing stream in the area north of Kos and the junction of the two currents is believed to have deposited the sand which has gradually raised the fringes of the Turkish coast and silted Kos harbour.

Laying-up Ports and Repairs. Yachts normally stay afloat during the winter months and may be moored by arrangement with the local authority at:

> Passalimani (Zea) ⎫
> Tourkolimano (Munychia) ⎬ Piraeus
> Vouliagmeni, 9 miles south of Piraeus
> Spetsai, 5 hours by ferry south of Piraeus.

Another port is Rhodes; and doubtless there are other places of which one could learn only by experience.

At the Piraeus ports refitting and slipping facilities are close at hand at Perama and arrangements may also be made for receiving yacht stores from England without paying duty. These ports therefore are the first choice. (See details under individual ports listed.)

Running Repairs. During a cruise it may be necessary to make good some misfortune which is beyond the scope of ship's resources. It is then a matter of chance whether or not outside help can be obtained. At many islands and small ports there is a boatbuilder, or a joiner's shop, or a mechanic in the village willing to help; sometimes quite unexpectedly one comes across a caique sailor who has experience in making sail repairs.

Note. The Greek National Tourist Organization now issues a chart denoting certain ports where repairs to a yacht can be undertaken, but one should realize that very few places in Greece have had previous experience with yacht work.

Berthing in Greek Ports. Normally yachts berth with an anchor laid out to seaward and stern to the quay. Some form of gang-plank is desirable.

This method of securing has certain advantages: the yacht's side does not get rubbed by the quay; one has some privacy from the gaze of onlookers; but perhaps more important still, one is less likely to be invaded by cockroaches or other vermin which sometimes frequent the quayside. In this unfortunate eventuality, the only successful way to eliminate the pest is to purchase 'Fumite' tablets made by Waeco Ltd., of Salisbury, Wilts, obtainable through Boots. Seal all apertures, ignite the tablets as directed and leave the yacht for 24 hours.

Note

All chart numbers quoted refer to British Admiralty charts. *Sailing Directions* refer to *Mediterranean Pilot*, Vol. IV.

WESTERN APPROACHES

to the AEGEAN

Scale |___|___|___| Miles
      0   10 20 30

Navarin Bay	Nymphi
Pylos	Kotronas
Methoni	Skutari Bay
Sapienza	Gythion
Gulf of Messenia	Xyli Bay
Koroni	Plythra
Kalamata	Elaphonisos Island
The Mani	Poriki Lagoon
Limeni	Vatica Bay
Mezapo	Vrakhonisos Petri
Gulf of Lakonia	Kithera Island
Asamato Cove	St Nikola
Vathy	Kapsali Bay
Port Kaio	Makri Cove
Kolokithia Bay	Panaghia
Meligani	Anti-Kithera Island
Solitare	Port Potamo

I

Western Approaches to the Aegean

From the southern shores of the Peloponnesus protrude three peninsulas forming the Gulfs of Messenia (or Kalamata) and Lakonia. Each gulf is of interest both for places of antiquity and for the few sheltered anchorages from which a shore excursion can be made.

This region is apt to be afflicted with boisterous weather and, especially in the case of a sailing yacht, it may therefore be useful to have full information on available shelter in the event of an emergency. Though north-westerly weather is usually associated with this area during the summer months, easterly or south-easterly gales sometimes occur in the spring, and it is then that a good port of refuge should be kept in mind.

NAVARINO AND PYLOS

A vessel approaching from the west and suddenly encountering adverse weather when south of the Peloponnesus would be well advised to make for Navarino if possible. This large bay is easy of access in bad weather and its sheltered small port of Pylos is of great historical interest.

Navarino Bay is sometimes used by British liners embarking Greek emigrants for Australia; they are brought to Pylos by road from Athens.

Pylos. Chart 211

Approach and Berth. On entering the bay, head for the extremity of Pylos breakwater—no difficulty day or night. Now turn into the port and lay out anchor to S.E. hauling in the stern to the mole. With easterly gales strong gusts sweep down the hilly slopes but the holding is good and the sea undisturbed. Only with S.W. gales is there a swell.

Facilities. There is a fresh water tap near the extremity of the mole, a number of fresh provision shops, one or two bars and restaurants and an attractive small modern hotel. Bus communications with Athens.

Earlier History. The earliest event recorded by Thucydides in his history of the Peloponnesian War was the 'Sphacteria Incident' in 425 B.C., when a small Athenian naval contingent under Demosthenes was left at Navarino as a thorn in the flesh to Sparta. But Spartan soldiers soon occupied the land around and besieged Demosthenes for some months in the heights of the Coryphasium peninsula. With the arrival of the main Athenian expedition, the besieging Spartans were themselves overwhelmed and a victorious fleet returned to Athens.

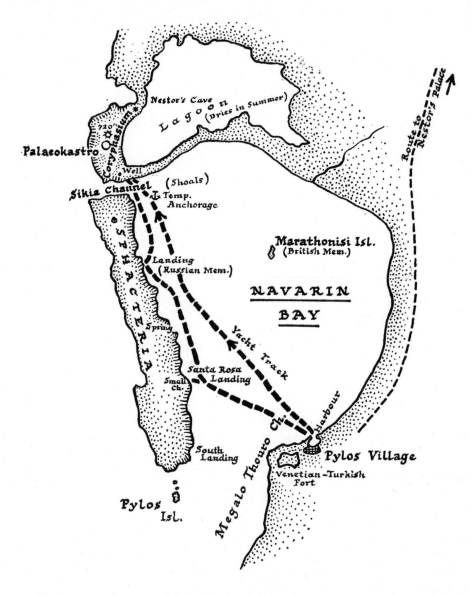

To investigate the scene of this early operation, one must proceed with the yacht to the sandy shore close to the shallow Sikia Channel, and anchor off the ancient port of Cory-phasium, whose mole can still be discerned disappearing among the rushes into the sand. From here a mule track ascends the 700-foot hill to the fortress on Palaeokastro. This was where Demosthenes detached himself from the Athenian expeditionary force bound for Syracuse and, having seized this peninsula with half a dozen triremes, set himself up for the

4

summer months to defy the besieging Spartans. Standing on the top today one looks down on the shallow channel where Demosthenes once sheltered his small squadron.

The existing fortress is of medieval construction, with battlemented walls in good preservation. From here there is also a magnificent view across the large semicircular bay of Navarino towards the green undulating country beyond.

Descending the steep northern slope, one soon comes to the stalactite cave where Hermes was reputed to have hidden the cattle he had stolen from Apollo. Inside the cave, when the cloud of bats has scattered, the glistening sides become visible, lit by a shaft of light from a hole high up in a dome roof giving a cathedral-like effect. By going on down from the cave, and proceeding along the shore by the dried-up lagoon one soon reaches the starting point.

It is impossible to anchor off the steep cliffs of Sphacteria, and one can only land by dinghy at 'Russian Cove' while the yacht is anchored elsewhere. From here a rough track ascends to the northern of the three peaks. This had been the Spartan stronghold until the return of the Athenian fleet from Syracuse when the tables were turned and the besiegers became the besieged. Demosthenes effected a landing, cut off Spartan supplies and eventually forced the surviving garrison to surrender. This dramatic and decisive conclusion to the campaign was never forgotten by the Athenians and for six centuries the Spartan shields were exhibited at Athens. On the hill-top today is the ruin of a small fort, but it is the setting itself which brings to life the events of the narrative so vividly told by Thucydides.

In 1827 an equally dramatic event took place which led to Greece obtaining her independence. The Turkish-Egyptian army was occupying the Peloponnesus and their fleet of 82 warships was at anchor in Navarino Bay. On 20 October an allied fleet of 27 warships including French and Russian ships, all commanded by Admiral Codrington, sailed into the bay. Owing to some trigger-happy Turkish ships firing at the boats of the allied fleet, Codrington's ships opened fire and, fighting fiercely throughout the day and most of the night, sank all but 29 of the enemy.

In the square at Pylos is the memorial, with busts of Codrington and his allied admirals, and on the island of Sphacteria, at Panagoulas, and on the islet of Chelonaki (Marathonisi) are small obelisks or modern plaques to commemorate the dead sailors of the French, Russian and British fleets respectively.

In order to look at the sunken Turkish ships of nearly 150 years ago, it is necessary to be equipped with skin-diving apparatus and descend to depths of 12 to 20 fathoms; but it is disappointing to find that the wrecks have been largely damaged by treasure-seeking parties half a century ago.

Apart from a well-preserved Turkish fort at the entrance to the bay, there is one further ancient site that should not be missed. This is Nestor's palace of about 1200 B.C., the foundations of which have only recently been excavated by Professor Blegen; it was here that many of the famous Linear B tablets were discovered.

Eight miles southward from Navarino is the south-westerly point of the Peloponnesus with the remains of a Venetian port, Methoni, behind it.

Methoni lies in a shallow bay, inadequately protected by a breakwater, with a modern village close by. A massive Venetian fortress jutting into the sea dominates the port.

The ancient walls of Methoni and Sapienza Island beyond

Approach and Berth. Charts 207 and 682 show there are no difficulties day or night. After rounding the extremity of the breakwater the sea bed rises very quickly. The most conspicuous object by day, not clearly shown on the chart, is the large Turkish tower on the southern point of the fortress. In fair weather only, a yacht may berth stern to the small quay 20 yards inside the mole with anchor laid out to the northward; the depths here are 10 feet—it may be preferable to anchor off, with the same shelter, in 2½ fathoms where there is good holding and sufficient swinging room. Bottom is thin weed on sand and there are a few stones. A swell works round the end of the mole and in bad weather from the south the place would be untenable.

In order to land at the castle or approach the village, one has to walk along the very rough 150-yard mole.

Port Facilities. Fresh water and fuel oil were being laid on to a small quay near the mole-head in 1961. The village is a poor place, lacking in the usual Greek conviviality. There is a café on the sea-front where a meal may be had. A fine sandy beach runs round the bay and this attracts a number of local visitors in the summer months. A road leads to Pylos. The place gives an impression of decay. Caiques and other vessels no longer call and only three or four small fishing craft are based here.

The vast Venetian fortress is worth a visit, though within the walls there is no building of interest remaining. The ancient port, now silted, can be seen to the southward of the existing mole.

In Venetian days this was one of the 'Eyes of the Republic' and because of its strategic position it became a relatively large port.

From the top of the Adriatic where 'Venice sat in state, throned on her hundred isles' the Pilgrim galleys under naval escort made voyages every year to the Holy Land. Methoni, which lay across their route, was invariably a port of call where oarsmen were rested and the vessels replenished with food and water before continuing the voyage via Chania, in Crete, on their passage to the Levant.

Protecting Methoni is the island of Sapienza with Port Longos as a suitable anchorage in southerly and westerly weather. This can be approached by day using only the southern entrance as the depths in the northern channel have become shallower than those charted, and one of the two rocky islets has disappeared.

The southern cove of the port is sandy and affords the best anchorage. There is a ruined building but no inhabitants on the island; only the lighthouse-keepers haul their boats up here.

In the seventeenth century sailing ships from England sometimes called here, and anchoring under the lee of Sapienza Island refilled their water casks at

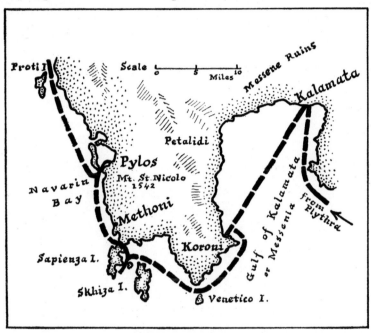

South-west Peloponnese. Navarin to Kalamata

Methoni. A warning in John Seller's *English Pilot* of 1677 states: 'Those that ride there must be sure to keep good watching lest your rigging and ropes be cut, for the Inhabitants of the place are very Thieves.'

It may be of interest that the rightful ownership of this insignificant deserted island was contested by the British government in the middle of the last century on the grounds of its having been a former Venetian possession and therefore must be surrendered to Britain. A British squadron was sent to Athens, and the threat of forceful measures was only prevented by the intervention of the distinguished traveller and Hellenophile, Colonel Leake. The claim was finally dropped.

7

GULF OF MESSENIA

Proceeding eastwards and passing beyond Venetico Island one enters the wide Gulf of Kalamata or Messenia. To the north-east and round the next headland is the other 'Eye of the Republic', **Koroni**—an elevated, walled city overlooking the small village with a reasonably sheltered anchorage behind a mole.

> **Approach and Berth.** Chart 207, with a small inset of the anchorage, shows the approach quite clearly by day or night. The fortress walls and bastions are visible a great distance off. 100 yards off the southern shore and up to 70 yards from the breakwater the bottom is short weed and sand. Farther out, and west of the extremity of the mole there are some rock slabs.
> The anchorage is slightly exposed to the afternoon day breeze from the north-west which may make boat landing rather a wet undertaking.
> **Port Facilities.** These are few, there being only one or two shops for provisions and a good taverna on the water-front.

The Venetian fortress, standing on the hill overlooking the village and port, is interesting to explore. The convent occupying part of the summit is inhabited by some nuns, who take great interest in maintaining a colourful flower garden.

An interesting excursion is a 20-minute drive through beautiful country to Petriades village. This is the only place in Greece where in the summer months the large 'Ali Baba' jars (amphorae) are made by hand without the aid of a potter's wheel, a process practised, apparently, only by this one family in the village.

Continuing past Koroni to the head of the Messenian Gulf you reach the relatively large commercial port of Kalamata—a very busy place in the autumn months when nearly three hundred steamers call to carry away the figs and currants. The inner basin is clean and well sheltered, and the town of fifty thousand people, reached by a frequent bus service, is a quarter of an hour distant; it has an interesting artisan quarter, some good shops and a small modern hotel.

A forty-minute drive inland brings one to a lengthy section of the massive walled defences of Messene. Raised against invasion by their hereditary enemy, the Spartans, in the middle of the fourth century B.C., these battlements, with their towers and gates still erect, can be followed on foot for a considerable distance over the hills. Despite earthquakes, these huge pieces of stone, neatly pieced together, mostly retain their perfect bonding today.

Kalamata

> **Approach and Berth.** Chart 682. The town is easily distinguished against the hinterland by day; but at night the harbour lights can be seen at only half the distance claimed.

After entering the port, a yacht should make for the north-west corner and berth in the basin with stern to the quay near the port office. Mud bottom, and depths of 28 feet nearly everywhere—good shelter.

Facilities. Fresh water, which is good, is laid on to the quay. Petrol and fuel oil are available close by.

A bus runs to Athens, three times a day, taking 10 hours. A fast train takes about the same time. There is also a daily air service to Athens.

Officials. This is a Port of Entry. Harbour Authority, Customs, Police, Immigration and Health.

The Mani. On the eastern shores of the Messenian Gulf is the rugged and largely barren coast of the tall Mani Peninsula. Its mountain ranges ascend to nearly 8,000 feet and exert a dominating influence on the winds inside these two gulfs. At the southern tip of the peninsula is the insignificant Cape Matapan (Ténaron to the Greeks). The eastern shores are inhospitable, and though Limeni is claimed to be a port for yachts, it is impossible to lie there comfortably in westerly winds.

From Limeni southwards a number of unusual villages with prominent square towers can sometimes be seen from seaward on the hill slopes. This is the country of the Deep Mani and these Nyklian towers were built from about 1600 onwards until the close of the eighteenth century. They were feudal strongholds built by the descendants of the former Nyklian families who came to the underpopulated Mani country on the destruction of their own city, Nykli, in Arcadia in 1295.

The towers, it seems, first grew up after the new settlers had occupied this lean and partially arable land. Refugees frequently entering, naturally sought land for themselves, and since it became largely a question of survival, the original settlers built these novel defences to deny further incursions on the land and into the villages. Usually of three stories, these towers may be seen both as a protection for the soil in the open country and for guarding the perimeters of villages. Because of the local vendettas, the village towers subsequently increased in number, each becoming a family stronghold. Some of them are still lived in, though in other places the whole village is largely deserted. Their appearance is more interesting than attractive.

The people nowadays are pleasant enough; but the traveller Wheler writing in 1675 calls them 'famous Pirates by sea, and Pestilent Robbers by land'; and Captain Beaufort 150 years later remarks:

'In the district of Maina, the Southern province of the Morea, there is a regularly organized system of absolute and general piracy. The number of their vessels or armed row-boats fluctuates between twenty and thirty; they lurk behind the headlands and innumerable rocks of the archipelago; all flags are equally their prey, and the life or death of the captured crew is merely a matter of convenience.'

Mezapo, southward of Limeni, is a small place lying in an open bay with a largely deserted village; and after rounding Cape Grosso with its impressive steep-to cliffs there is Gerolimena with a quay and a few houses, where the steamer calls once a week.

Apart from a call at Koroni a visit by sailing yacht into this gulf is hardly justified.

GULF OF LAKONIA

Rounding the uninspiring Cape Matapan and entering the Gulf of Lakonia, there are some attractive places on the mountainous steep-to Mani shores, but apart from one or two coves shown in the plans on Chart 1685 and Port Kaio on Chart 3342 there are hardly any safe places to leave a sailing yacht for more than an hour or two. This is largely on account of the squalls which may at any time descend with violence from the steep Mani ranges above.

Asamato Cove is comfortable in settled weather, when a yacht should anchor in the north-west corner of the bay with a warp to the shore. The bottom here is inconveniently deep and shelves quickly. There is only a fisherman's hut at the head of the creek. This cove is less subject to squalls than other places in this area.

Vathy is a deep-cut inlet often claimed to be better than Asamato, though subject to violent squalls in westerly winds.

Port Kaio. Chart 3342 (plan). This is the best shelter near Matapan. Usually a yacht anchors in the southern creek in 5 fathoms on a sandy bottom, where there is plenty of room to swing and the holding appears good; but being open to N.E. it is sometimes advisable during adverse conditions to shelter in the northern creek close under the conspicuous monastery on the hillside.

There is no convenient place to land in the dinghy in the event of a short sea, and one must be content with the beach close to some newly built cottages. The 'towered' village, half an hour's walk up the hill, is hardly worth the ascent, for most of the houses are deserted. In 1961 only thirty people still lived here and two nuns were the sole inhabitants of the monastery above the opposite creek.

A walk to the lighthouse on Cape Matapan takes an hour: the famous cave—

the entrance to Hades—nearby is reached by following a goat-track passing through the low scrub which covers most of the hillside.

In this wild, open country thousands of quail may sometimes be seen. In April they are northbound, often calling at Aegean islands. In September they may be seen taking off for Africa, preferring to make the 200-mile sea flight at night.

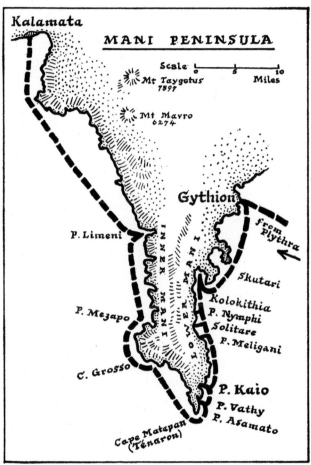

Kolokithia Bay. Continuing into this bay, one notices its delightful green slopes and attractive valleys, yet there are no places, with the exception of Gythion, where one would dare to leave a sailing yacht at anchor for more than an hour or two unless the weather was very settled. The following places are mostly small and rather exposed:

Meligani—a small bay, with a few houses, open to the east.

Solitare—similar to the above, but more used by small caiques.

Nymphi—a narrow rocky inlet 150 yards long with an open beach, and open only to the east.

Kotronas lies in a most delightful setting in a small bay with a quay (6 feet); anchorage is in 5 fathoms; close in there are stones on the bottom. Ashore there are a few houses and a taverna—a few fishing boats use the place. As this anchorage is so susceptible to the violent gusts from the hills, a small quay has been built into the rocks about 400 yards southward, where caiques usually anchor for better shelter.

Skutari Bay has lovely scenery, but there is no anchorage for a yacht—it is liable to strong mountain gusts.

Gythion. Chart 3351 (plan). A pleasant deserted old port with a decaying small town—useful for making excursions to Sparta and Mistra.

Approach and Berth. Chart 3342 shows that there are no difficulties day or night, and a yacht should make for the Inner Harbour. Secure stern to the mole with anchor to the westward in depths of 2 fathoms—bottom is firm clay. Though the harbour appears to be reasonably sheltered it can in fact be dangerous for a vessel to lie here during strong north-west winds on account of the violent gusts from the Taygetus Mountains. Easterly winds bring in a swell.

Port Facilities. Fresh water of poor quality is available by hydrant from the quay. Diesel fuel is also obtainable from the quay and petrol from Shell on the quayside. There are ample provision shops with fruit and vegetables; two or three old-fashioned hotels and two restaurants. The Piraeus steamer calls twice a week; there is a daily bus to Athens (9 hours) and two or three buses a day to Sparta.

The population of Gythion is still declining, there being little employment here and in the neighbourhood. Many Greek tourists come for the bathing in the summer months.

The sea walls of the ancient port may be seen under water close off the outflow of the stream north of the town.

A newly-constructed road, passing over the mountains and through attractive green cultivated country, enables buses to reach Sparta in an hour. This is a modern town of little interest; but Mistra, 15 minutes further, is a most interesting Byzantine city standing under the Taygetus ranges, with many churches and convents still in good order. It is well worth a whole day's visit.

Plythra, the port of Xyli Bay, is shown on Chart 1436. Protected by a long breakwater it is a dreary, barren little place.

Approach and Berth. The depth off the breakwater in the approach channel is 12 feet and the bottom uneven rocks. By night a hand lantern is exhibited on the mole-head. Berth not more than 30 yards inside the mole-head with stern to quay, bows northward. Bottom is uneven rock, boulders and gravel. Above- and below-water rocks lie only 60 yards north of the mole. It is not a safe harbour.

Facilities. Very limited provisions to be bought at the hamlet. No good fresh water available. There is the Government Pavilion for a few tourists in summer. Buses run daily to Sparta.

The port was constructed for the shipment of figs from the hinterland and is used in the autumn months. The ancient town lies submerged near the root of the mole.

Elaphonisos Island, only 12 miles farther south, has its village on the eastern end of the boat channel. A fine lagoon is formed on the island's western side by a low line of rocks (Poriki) sheltering the anchorage from all weather except strong westerly winds, but there is nothing of interest ashore.

Vatica Bay, throughout history, has provided shelter during hostilities for the warships of every nation endeavouring to control the western approaches to the Aegean; in early days Roman and Venetian galleys were stationed here, and in each of the recent World Wars both British and German patrol vessels. Neapolis, a large village on the north-eastern corner, is a calling place for the steamer; it affords but little shelter for a yacht. In fact, except for an excellent lee close under its shores, especially in Vrakhonisos Petri (N.W. corner), this bay is not recommended for a yacht under normal conditions.

South of Elaphonisos Island is the 4½-mile wide Elaphonisos Channel separating it from Kithera Island. This channel provides the main route for vessels entering the Aegean from the west.

> *Forsaken isle! around thy barren shore*
> *Wild tempests howl and wintry surges roar.*
> WRIGHT (*Horae Ionicae,* 1807).

Kithera Island is mountainous and steep-to with a barren-looking coast. There are two sheltered bays: St Nikolo (Avlemona) on the south-eastern corner of the island, and Kapsali Bay with the Chora (capital or main village) on the south coast. Plans are given on Chart 1685.

There are also two places of shelter on the north-east coast, suitable only under favourable conditions: Panaghia with its 100-yard breakwater and the sandy lagoon of Makri.

St Nikolo (on British charts) is a name unknown to the Greeks, who call the place **Avlemona.** This is the safest harbour in the island, sheltered in all weather, though open to southerly swell.

13

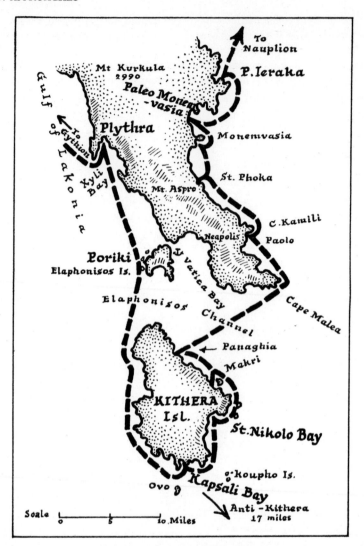

Elos Peninsula and Kithera Island

Berth. A small quay with depths of 3 fathoms is sometimes occupied by caiques, otherwise it is the most suitable place for securing a yacht's sternfast, with her anchor laid out to the southward. The basins are small, there is swinging room if desiring to anchor in the outer basin in depths of 3 or 4 fathoms.

Though the configuration of the port is attractive, the barrenness of the surrounding country and the poor decaying hamlet make no appeal for a visiting yacht.

There was an occasion, however, in Nelson's day when the approach to this little harbour was causing much concern:

On 17 September 1802 the small brig *Mentor* conveying 17 cases of the famous Parthenon frieze was on passage to Malta; seeking shelter from a westerly gale she put in at St Nikolo Bay. Her two anchors began to drag, and in trying to make sail she cut her cables but drifted on the rocks and was holed; she sank in 60 feet close off shore, the crew managing to reach the rocky coast, all being saved. It was two years before divers from Kalimnos and Symi (whose sailors continue this vocation today) were able to complete their task, and retrieve all these cases from the wreck. Finally on 16 February 1805 the transport *Lady Shaw Stewart*, under orders of Lord Nelson, called at St Nikolo, loaded the cases and conveyed them to England.

As well as the Elgin marbles, this stormy sea had formerly taken a toll of Greek sculptures conveyed in Roman ships, many of which had been wrecked on their way to Italy. Thanks to the efforts of Greek sponge-divers in recent years a few of the Athens Museum's greatest treasures have been recovered from the sea bed off Kithera.

Kapsali Bay. Shown in a plan on Chart 1685, it lies in a mountainous setting with an anchorage open to the south; it is dominated by a massive Venetian castle. The Chora, (capital of the island) lies 600 feet up and is one of the most attractive little towns in Greece.

Approach and Berth. A yacht can either anchor in the bay in 4 fathoms or berth (with caution) behind the rocky spur on which the lighthouse stands, and where shelter is better. The new quay has a depth of only 8 feet, but is useful for securing a sternfast when the yacht has laid out an anchor to the westward. The sea bottom in the anchorage is sand, but near the quay among patches of sand are loose rock and stones, giving uncertain holding. The bay is susceptible to a swell, and untenable only in Sirocco winds. In the summer months westerly winds predominate, with an occasional spell of north-easterly weather.

Port Facilities. Fresh water, which is good, is available from a tap near the quayside, and in 1961 was being piped to the quay which was itself being improved to provide fuel oil. Petrol can be bought at one of the few houses in the port; also limited provisions.

The Chora, a full half hour's walk up a steep hill, lies in a commanding position beyond the Venetian castle. Its winding, fascinating streets with well-stocked shops are remarkably clean and neat. Good fish, including crayfish, are often obtainable there and in the port; there is a modest hotel and restaurant. People are friendly everywhere and tourists unknown. There are one or two motor drives to the other villages in the centre of the island.

The island continues to export some palatable Retsina for which it was once famous.

The Piraeus steamer calls twice a week. For many years there has been a meteorological station here, and one may still obtain a useful forecast.

In earlier days this island was regarded as a watch-post for the gateway to the

Aegean. After the Napoleonic wars Kithera, together with the Ionian Islands, was ceded to Britain, and was garrisoned by a small detachment under a subaltern's command. The garrison was relieved every six months, it being considered 'a very lonely station'. Some English cannon, a bridge and a few graves are the only remains of this British occupation.

Though caiques and small mail-boats sometimes land passengers at Makri Cove and at Panaghia on the east coast, neither is recommended, the former having but little interest and the latter no dependable shelter.

The island of **Anti-Kithera** lies between Kithera and Crete. The 10-mile wide navigable channels on either side of it are used by vessels proceeding in the direction of Crete.

Anti-Kithera has a rocky inlet with a hamlet on the north, Port Potamo, shown on chart 1685. It is seldom visited, largely because of the heavy swell which comes in during fresh northerly winds.

Across the Anti-Kithera channel, on the north-west coast of Crete, is the inhospitable anchorage of Grabousa (see chapter 6, Crete), but the nearest safe port is Souda Bay.

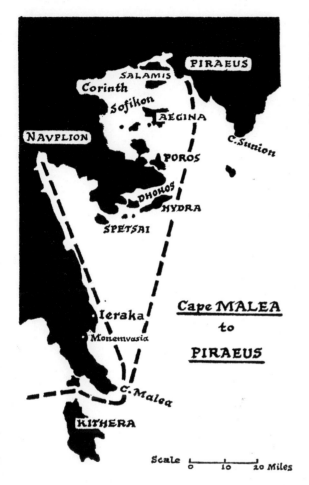

Cape Malea
Port Paolo
St Phoka
Monemvasia
Paleo Monemvasia
Port Ieraka
Port Kyparisa
Port Phokianos
Gulf of Argolis
Scala Leonidhion
Astros
Nauplion
Tolos
Khaidhari
Koiladhi
Port Cheli
Kosta
Spetsai
Spetsapoula
Dhokos
Ermione
Idhra
Poros
Aegina
Palaia Epidavros
Sofikon
Corinth Canal
Salamis
Cape Konkhi
Piraeus
Passalimani
Tourkolimano
Vouliagmeni

2

Western Shores of the Aegean

PART I: *CAPE MALEA TO PIRAEUS*

Slowly sinks more lovely ere his race be run
Along Morea's hills, the setting sun;
Not, as in Northern climes, obscurely bright,
But one unclouded blaze of living light.

BYRON

EAST COAST OF PELOPONNESUS

Cape Malea, the bold mountainous headland rising to nearly 2,000 feet, forms the turning point into the Aegean. Completely isolated and standing on the hillside close westward a few hundred feet above the sea stands a low, white monastery now inhabited by half a dozen nuns.

With westerly winds the cape should be rounded, keeping at least a mile off, especially when turning northwards towards the Gulf of Argolis.

This noble headland makes a profound impression, and to the ancient Greek sailors on a long voyage to some distant colony it was perhaps the last they were to see of their own country for many months to come. 'Round Malea and forget your native country' was the saying attributed to these early sailors. Many centuries later, shortly after the hey-day of Venice, small vessels of the British Levant Company,* after a voyage of 6 or 7 weeks from England, used, in their turn, to round this Cape into the Aegean. Shipping cargoes mainly at Constantinople and Smyrna, they also visited the Port of Lions (Piraeus) and Monemvasia; but the Aegean islands, except perhaps Chios, were of no interest for trading purposes. Having entered the 'Arches' (a corruption of archipelago) they called at Milos for a pilot, and sometimes an armed naval escort, for the Aegean was then a hunting ground for pirates.

* The French, more successful in the Levant, had as many as 700 vessels in this trade shortly before the Napoleonic Wars.

Today the shipping activity off Cape Malea is nothing compared with that off such headlands as St Vincent and Europa Point.

Cape Malea to Cape Sabbatiki

From Cape Malea northwards a 2,000-foot mountainous spur stands steeply above the coast; the foothills are partially cultivated. There are some small villages concealed in the valleys. Only indifferent shelter can be found before reaching Monemvasia and Ieraka.

Port Paolo lies 1½ miles W.S.W. from Cape Kamili. It is a very small fishing cove with 12-foot depths protected by a 50-yard mole extending in a southerly direction from the northern shore; a very small white church at the root of the mole makes an excellent sea mark. The cove should be used only in settled weather, and it is susceptible to an easterly swell. There is no habitation apart from a small farm and the hamlet 2 or 3 miles distant. Except for some cultivated valleys and noble mountains there is nothing of particular interest.

St Phoka is 5 miles south of Monemvasia, and consists of a very small inlet behind an islet. It can be recognized from seaward by the few houses of the hamlet, and the islet by its small church. The approach is in a north-westerly direction, leaving the islet with its protruding underwater rocks to starboard. The channel is narrow with 2-fathom depths, and on no account should a vessel attempt to enter in the event of an easterly swell, which can be seen breaking on the rocks. Within the inlet there is just room to swing in 2 fathoms.

Monemvasia. A small Gibraltar-like headland is joined to the mainland by a causeway. This acts as a breakwater and affords temporary anchorage either north or south according to the weather.

Anchorage. Either side the holding is poor, but the most convenient place to anchor is 80 yards from the western shore and 80 yards from the bridge. The bottom here is flat rock with sandy patches and small boulders in a depth of 7 fathoms. In the event of unsettled weather it is advisable to anchor in the bay of Paleo Monemvasia 2½ miles northward.

Facilities. The stone landing-pier at the eastern end of the Causeway leads to the new village of over a thousand people. Here there are shops with fresh provisions, wine, post office and ice store. Water is obtainable only from cisterns in the private houses. In the Venetian village on the Rock only a few of the old houses are inhabited; but there is a restaurant for tourists and a taverna.

There is regular steamer communication with Piraeus twice weekly (7 or 8 hours), and a daily bus service to Athens. Cruise steamers often put in here for a few hours.

The peninsula with its walled Venetian town is worth visiting, and the Byzantine church of St Sophia on the summit even more so. From here the outer walls of the fortifications are impressive and lend support to the stories of the many sieges this stronghold has withstood.

Monemvasia was also a centre of commerce famous in medieval days for its Malmsey* wines, which were of wide repute. Here the jars of wine were assembled from places on the Morea coast and from some of the islands to await onward shipment to Western Europe, including England.

Paleo Monemvasia. A small sheltered bay with depths of 3 to 5 fathoms over an irregular smooth rock and sandy bottom. This is a much better place for a yacht than Monemvasia in unsettled weather.

> **Anchorage.** The two wrecks shown on Chart 1436 have largely dispersed; one lying in 3 fathoms 120 yards off the cottages is no longer dangerous to ships, though there might be some risk of its fouling a vessel's cable.
> **Facilities.** There are half-a-dozen fishermen's cottages and a small taverna where basic provisions may be obtained. A road goes to Monemvasia—an hour's walk.

Port Ieraka. This is the best sheltered and most pleasant port between Cape Malea and Spetsai.

> **Anchorage.** Chart 1436. This is well protected by the configuration of the steep coast; the only inconvenience is the occasional down-currents of wind under certain conditions. One should anchor in 5 fathoms rather than get into lesser depths, when the bottom becomes too hard for a plough anchor to be sure of holding.

A few cottages of the hamlet line the water-front at the foot of the steep sides of the anchorage. The steamer from Piraeus calls twice a week.

Port Kyparisa. An anchorage off a small village lying in a spacious bay at the foot of steep, wooded mountains. Though open to the east and subject to strong down-draughts during westerly winds, there are convenient depths for anchoring off a small quay. This place is suitable only in settled weather.

Port Phokianos. This is a large, deep inlet in the mountainous coast with a few deserted houses at its head. It is an unsuitable anchorage.

GULF OF ARGOLIS

Entering the Gulf between Cape Sambateki and Spetsai, some of the small ports and anchorages only a few miles apart are of interest to a yacht.

* Corruption of Monemvasia.

Local Winds. Under fine weather conditions the day breeze blows from the S.E. up the gulf, starting before midday. There is a light breeze beginning before dawn and lasting until about 10 o'clock, blowing down the gulf from the N.W. With fresh westerly winds the mountainous shores of the gulf are subject to down-blasts, and the coast should be passed with an offing of about 3 miles. In some of the ports at the top of the Gulf the more violent squalls may set up a series of miniature tidal waves. With a rise and fall of 1 to 2 feet they may occur at few-minute intervals and can be embarrassing to yachts secured with stern warps to a quay.

West Side of Gulf

Scala Leonidhion. Chart 1518. This small port for Leonidhion village has a short mole affording poor shelter. Though of no interest to yachts, the Piraeus steamer and caiques call here to collect passengers and produce from the hinterland.

Astros. A pleasant, small fishing port well protected by an 80-yard mole—a good summer anchorage—and only untenable in the winter during S.E. gales.

Berth. Nearly 2-fathom depths extend towards the extremity of the mole, but along the waterfront the harbour has largely silted. A yacht can berth stern to the quay, anchor towards the village.

Though only a poor little village it has a small restaurant, and a modest hotel was being built in 1961. Daily bus service to Nauplia and Athens, and southward to Leonidhion.

A delightful half hour's drive takes one to the Byzantine monastery of Moni Loukas on the mountainside.

Nauplion lies at the head of the gulf and is a pleasant town with much of historical interest close by. Formerly a small commercial port, this place has recently become a tourist centre. The harbour and town are clean and interesting, and the port reasonably well-sheltered in the summer months. It merits a stay of 2 or 3 days.

Approach and Berth. Chart 1308. The harbour is spacious and easy of access. The 'day breeze', setting in about noon blows up the Gulf from the S.S.E. and is inclined to be gusty from the high land off the port. At night there is often a land breeze.

During settled conditions it is convenient to berth in the eastern corner of the western basin opposite the Hotel Grand Bretagne, with stern to quay and bows N.N.W. In the event of N.W. squalls from the Arcadian Mountains it is advisable to move into the inner basin, where the quay is surprisingly clean.

These squalls sometimes cause a surge in the port abreast the quays, when it is necessary to slacken off the stern warps.

Facilities. Everything can be bought locally and the shops are close at hand. Local piped water is not good, but drinking water is sold from a lorry which tours the town.

The old Venetian Fort Bourdzi, with a quick ferry service to the quay, has been turned into an hotel-restaurant. Two large modern hotels have been built in 1961, one lying on the saddle with splendid views. In the town are several smaller hotels and restaurants of varying category.

Officials. Nauplion is a Port of Entry and consequently has the full quota of officials.

The Venetian citadel on the summit of Palamide, approached by 857 steps, is worth the ascent, especially on a clear day when the views across the Argos Plain are magnificent. In the town there are many houses in Venetian style and a museum of limited interest.

There are interesting day excursions by car or bus to Tiryns, Argos, Mycenae and Epidaurus; also reasonably quick communication by bus and rail with Athens.

When Greece first obtained her independence in 1832 Nauplion became for a short while the first capital of the country, Athens at this time being a village of little significance.

East Side of Gulf

Tolos. A partially sheltered anchorage protected by an island off the 'seaside' village of Tolos.

Anchorage. Many fishing boats moor off, there being no harbour; with northerly winds the anchorage is susceptible to strong gusts off the hills. There are convenient depths of about 3 fathoms with good holding about 100 yards offshore.

This village, only 12 kilometres from Nauplion, has become a minor resort with two small hotels, some modest restaurants and shops.

East of the village are some ruins on the promontory. This is ancient Asine whose harbour is now silted and filled with sand; from here Agamemnon's expedition set off for Troy.

Khaidhari. A sheltered inlet near the ruins of Mezes. The sea bed rises sharply-at the head of the bay to 2 fathoms. No village—rather bleak and steep hills either side of the inlet, causing strong gusts with N.W. winds.

Koiladhi is the port for the large village of Kranidhi, and lies in a sheltered bay whose entrance is difficult to discern. Here is a small, primitive village, mostly inhabited by fishermen; though there was no fresh water in 1961, piping was about to be laid on.

Anchorage. The best anchorage is off the S.E. point of the village in 2 fathoms. With northerly winds a slight swell enters the port; but in this shallow anchorage holding is good and the sea breeze steady.

Port Cheli (or Kheli) is a large enclosed bay with a dull little village.

Anchorage. Anchor N.E. of the village quay and swing or lay out the anchor northwards and haul in the stern. There is 10 feet depth at the quay. Fresh water is available from a tap at this Quay and at the 'Fish Quay', but it is inclined to be brackish at both places.

There is a modest hotel with a restaurant close to the quay. A bus service operates between here and Nauplia, connecting also with Epidaurus.

Kosta. An open sandy bay with short jetty, it is the mainland terminal for Spetsai. People leave their motor-cars here and cross the strait ($1\frac{1}{2}$ miles) by caique to Spetsai. There is a taverna on the shore by the jetty. Excellent for bathing, and in summer a fair temporary anchorage, though the bay is entirely open to the south-east.

Spetsai. Chart 1518. It is a hilly island, wooded on the north, well known to Athenians as a summer resort. There are two harbours: the Boat Harbour off the village centre where the Piraeus ferry calls, and **Balza** (a creek at the N.E. end of the island) which is suitable for yachts, berthing, servicing and laying-up.

Approach and anchorage for Balza. The lighthouse stands out fairly well and the port may be approached by day or night—see plan on page 25.

Yachts usually anchor the S.W. side of the lighthouse off a small stone pier in depths of $2\frac{1}{2}$ fathoms. This is open to N.W. and a swell sometimes rolls in, but the holding is good. Land at stone pier in dinghy—8 minutes' walk to the village.

Berth in the Inner Harbour. There is a quay (with shallow depths close in) where caiques berth and work their cargoes. Towards the head of the creek there is usually more room, though it is necessary to berth well away from the quay. Here are a few suitable berths for small yachts (up to 20 tons) to lay up for the winter, where shelter is better than at most Aegean ports.

Port Facilities. Provisions may be bought nearby from a caique that brings them across from the mainland. The large hotel 'Poseidonion' and several smaller ones, also restaurants, are all 10 minutes' walk from Balza and close by the Boat Harbour. Water can be obtained from the quay: also diesel fuel, petrol and paraffin.

When laying-up a yacht here it is essential to realize that during the winter months the sea level drops about $2\frac{1}{2}$ feet.

A large finishing school for boys lies to the westward of the hotel, both buildings being conspicuous when approaching from the west. Most of the villas are empty in the winter months, and only the small local population remains.

There are two small shipyards where local caiques are built and small yacht

AEGEAN HARBOURS

The yacht basin at Tourkolimano

Hydra

The island of Crete: the elevated plain of Lassithi

Patmos: the harbour

To Boat Harbour

Lt.F(R)
Lt.Tower
(Small)

To SPETSAI
village

Lt.Occ.

Lt.Ho.
(Conspic)

Approach
Course

Ch.

Boat
Quay

Rising Ground

Yacht
anchorage

Quay

16
Fishing
Quay   14

Shallow

Sheds

15

Slipways

15

14

Slipway

Caiques

Church
(on skyline)

N

Q
U
A
Y

11 13

11 14

Yacht

18

Buildings
Shed

Slipways

Balza Creek, Spetsai. (*Soundings in feet.*)

repairs can be undertaken, including the slipping of a yacht up to 7 feet draft. The technical resources on the island are limited.

There are no motor-cars, but a few horse-drawn gharries.

Spetsapoula. A small island S.E. of Spetsai with a yacht harbour which is privately owned by Mr Stavros Niarchos, the Greek ship-owner.

THE NEAR ISLANDS

These islands lie within 50 miles of Piraeus, which can be reached by ferry steamer in 3 or 4 hours. They are sometimes referred to by modern writers as the Saronic Islands. Chart 1518 shows the main island of Idhra (or Hydra) and Poros, and the coast beyond the Methana Peninsula.

The 'Near' or Saronic Islands

Before entering the Idhra Strait there is the uninhabited and largely barren island of **Dhokos** with two partially sheltered coves on the northern side, suitable as a temporary yacht anchorage. There is also on the mainland the shallow little port of **Ermione** with its adjoining hamlet connected to the main road system. Though pleasant for a night anchorage, none of these places is recommended for a special visit.

Idhra or **Hydra** is a long barren island with a central spur rising to 2,000 feet. Its interest lies in the picturesque small port, where almost the whole of the island's 3,000 population live. The unusual architecture of the attractively built houses of early Hydriot families rise one above the other as though forming an amphitheatre round the three sides of the harbour.

Approach and Berth. The entry is straightforward day or night, and a yacht should berth off the main quay near the church, or if this is congested with caiques (as it sometimes is in summer) berth stern to the breakwater. Though appearing to be a well-sheltered port it can, in fact, be very disturbed in N.W. winds, and Hydra is certainly not such a safe harbour as Spetsai.

Facilities. It is easy to step ashore on the clean broad quay where all the shops are, and to find a wide choice of fresh provisions (brought across from the mainland). Fresh water is very scarce. There are a number of restaurants on the quay, some modest hotels and a bathing place on the rocks outside the harbour. Small repairs can be done by a yard that builds local motor-boats. A school of navigation stands above the steamer quay where the Piraeus steamer calls 3 or 4 times daily in summer—a 3-hour passage; also a hydrofoil boat calls.

Apart from the little church of Ayios Ioannis (with original frescoes) close above the town, the only excursion is an hour's climb to the monastery of Prophitis Ilias. It stands high on the mountain, and a mule can be hired.

Though the monastery is uninhabited and without interest except for its bell-tower, the neighbouring convent is attractive and well maintained by a few nuns. It affords a magnificent view.

Though crowded with tourists in summer during the day, Hydra is a colourful little port much animated by the gaily-painted caiques unloading their produce, and by the arrival of the fast ferry-boats from Piraeus embarking and disembarking passengers many times in the day. By night the place quietens down, for the tourists have left, and only those with summer villas and the local people remain.

Earlier History. From the harbour looking up at the houses it is at once apparent that many of them were built for people of wealth and, except for Spetsai, have nothing in common with the humble dwellings on other islands. Relatively large and constructed of a grey stone now weathered, they are usually approached by a small garden with shrubs through which can be seen a panelled door with a richly moulded knocker. On the seaward side is a loggia standing on the steep parapet with a commanding view over the port.

They were built in the eighteenth century by Albanian familes, who migrated here at the time of Turkish suppression, and by the latter part of that century had developed a maritime trade with many parts of the Mediterranean. A large number of sailing craft were built here; schooners and brigs were soon earning big profits.

27

When the War of Independence broke out in the early twenties of the next century, these families put their ships at the disposal of the newly-formed Greek Navy. At that time there were 4,000 seamen on the island, and about 150 ships of which no fewer than 80 were of 300 tons burden or more; most of them well manned and armed.

History has handed down accounts of spirited actions against Turkish warships. On one occasion they captured a Turkish corvette and decided to name her after the island; she thus became the first *Hydra* of the Greek Navy.

Some Hydriot leaders have been highly praised for their part in the War, especially Admiral Miaoulis whose statue now stands outside the church, and other Greek patriots such as Tombazi and Condouriotis, whose descendants still own their original family houses.

Commerce recovered after the War and thrived well into the latter part of the last century. The presence of bollards and mooring facilities in the more sheltered coves of Hydra and Spetsai reveal where these schooners and brigs were laid up in the winter months.

Poros is an attractive, land-locked bay sometimes used as a Fleet anchorage. It is a pleasant place to visit in a yacht; the green shores with one or two coves are attractive and the small town is pleasant.

Approach. Chart 1657. The northern entrance can take unlimited draft; but the tortuous eastern channel, which is used by the Piraeus ferry-steamers, must be treated with caution. Here the northern shore must be followed within 100 feet in certain places—see sketch.

Anchorage. It will be noted that the 10-fathom sea bed rises sharply at the sides to 3 fathoms or less. In the event of a blow, it might be necessary for a yacht to shift to the best lee available, but normally a yacht should anchor in 2 or 3 fathoms, about 100 yards from the ferry quay in the Poros Strait, yet clear of the fairway.

Note. The Inner Harbour, which according to the British chart is being dredged to 12 feet, has in fact barely 6 feet and is used exclusively by naval boats. It is, however, possible to anchor

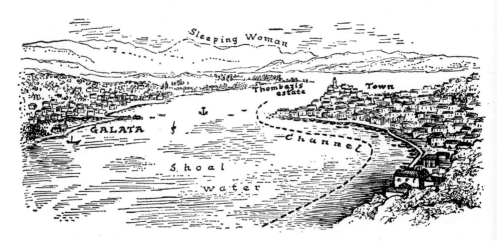

View from the eastern entrance to Poros looking towards N.W.

in the small coves on the north side of Poros Bay, which, though somewhat far from the town, are claimed to be fairly sheltered and afford pleasant anchorage.

Port Facilities. Water may be obtained from a tap alongside south of the ferry quay, but it is advisable to go to a pipe line on a light pier projecting from the Thombazi estate, half a mile N.W. of Galata. The depth at the pierhead is only 9 feet; but the water is excellent and permission may usually be obtained by calling upon the caretaker of the estate if the landlord is absent.

There is an ice factory at Galata, where petrol and diesel fuel may be bought, as well as on the island itself.

Summer hotels and some reasonably attractive restaurants are close to the steamer landing place. A tourist hotel with bathing place has been built outside the town, being approached by the one and only road, a couple of miles distant from the main quay.

A steamer service during the summer months connects with Piraeus via Aegina, taking about 3 hours. There is also a less frequent service to Hydra and Spetsai.

A small naval hospital will always help in an emergency.

The monastery and the ruins of the temple of Poseidon are worth a visit. The monastery can be reached by bus or taxi in 15 minutes and also by motor-boat, and the ruins of the temple are an hour's walk above the monastery—mostly through pinewoods.

An interesting visit can be made to Troezen where in 1827 the first meeting of the Greek National Assembly was held, and Cabo D'Istria was elected president. Troezen can be reached either by bus from Galata, or by 40 minutes' easy going on foot from Vidhi, a poor anchorage at the western end of Poros Bay. Though the ruins of the temple of Hippolyte and the Byzantine church are fragmentary, the mountain views across the fertile plain are magnificent.

Aegina (now spelt **Aiyina** on Admiralty charts and **Egina** on Greek charts). This is a hilly island, cultivated in places, with a well-sheltered though shallow little port—a seaside resort for Athenians.

Approach and Berth. Chart 1657 (plan). The leading marks as charted are difficult to discern, but the approach course 071° leads through a channel with just under 2 fathoms depths into the harbour. There is 2 fathoms within 50 yards of the ferry-steamer quay and 1½ fathoms close to the quayside. It is advisable to berth within this limit, as the further parts of the harbour shoal to 6 feet. The bows of a yacht should therefore, be pointed to seaward before 'letting go' and the stern hauled in towards the quay.

Port Facilities. There are provision shops and a fish market close by. Petrol may be obtained from a pump, and ice is available. Water is not easily come by; but it can be obtained by water-cart rather expensively. Taxis are available. There are one or two modest hotels; a palatable white wine may be bought locally.

The small town of Aegina is unattractive; the island, though green in early summer and partly wooded, dries up in the hot weather.

There is steamer communication with Piraeus three or four times a day, and with Poros, Hydra, Spetsai and Leonidhion.

Though the local museum is hardly worth a visit, the drive to the Doric temple of Aphaia is picturesque and the temple very fine. For a yacht, this may be better visited from Ayia Marina Bay. Though open and entirely exposed to the S.E. quadrant, this bay is attractively situated and much frequented by yachts from Piraeus. From the hamlet on the shore, nowadays visited by many tourists, a path leads up to the temple of Aphaia an easy half hour's walk.

Historical. Looking at Aegina today it is difficult to imagine it in the middle of the fifth century B.C. when it had grown strong enough, both militarily and commercially, to be a rival to Athens. The Athenians attacked it, but only after a four years' siege by their fleet was the island captured and its population deported. Nearly two thousand years later Aegina suffered a worse catastrophe when the pirate Barbarossa overran the Aegean islands. In Aegina he butchered the men and carried off six thousand women and children. When the French fleet put in here soon afterwards their admiral reported he could find no people living on the island.

Palaia Epidavros is a charming anchorage at the foot of the Peloponnese mountains with an interesting approach.

Approach and Berth. Unfortunately Charts 1514 and 1517 which gave such useful detail have been withdrawn and only the small scale Chart 1518 is available. The leading marks through the narrow approach channel are still described in *Sailing Directions*, the passage through the Narrows now being facilitated by port and starboard lighted buoys.

Either anchor in 2 to 3 fathoms in the middle of the bay or berth off the quay, recently extended, and having 10 feet depths close off. By night a light is now established at the corner of the quay.

Facilities. The village of 500 people has little to offer apart from fruit and vegetable shops. There is a small inn; a bus runs daily to Nauplia; a few caiques call.

It is possible to hire a taxi for the drive to the theatre at *Epidaurus*—the finest in all Greece less than an hour along a good road.

Continuing in a N.N.W. direction, close under the tall mountainous coast there is a well-sheltered bay with a small attractive village:

Sofikon, an attractive bay in mountainous surroundings.

Approach and Anchorage. Chart 1657. After avoiding obstructions both outside and at the entrance, anchor in the N.E. corner of the bay, off the eastern end of the village, in 3 or 4 fathoms. Shelter is all-round.

The hamlet has only three shops.

In the N.W. corner of the Gulf of Athens (Saronic Gulf) lies the undiscernible entrance to the Corinth Canal at Kalamaki. As the Gulf narrows, a mountain with medieval fortifications stands out prominently in the distance. This is Acro-Corinth and, though it lies on the west side of the Corinth Canal, it is the best distant mark for the Canal approach; the Canal entrance cannot be discerned until one is almost there.

Corinth Canal. Chart 1600. A yacht wishing to leave the Aegean and pass through the Canal is sometimes met by an official in a launch; but if not, it is advisable to go alongside the rickety jetty where an official may come on board to calculate the Canal dues. For a 20-ton yacht this may amount to about £7, which is more expensive than the charges at Kiel, Suez or Panama. One then waits for the Red Flag to be hauled down, when the yacht may proceed through the Canal under power without having to take a pilot. This dull 3-mile cut passes between vertical limestone cliffs 250 feet high on either side. The Canal, 80 feet wide and 26 feet deep, is much used by caiques and local steamers which thus save a distance of 140 miles on the sea route round the Peloponnesus via Matapan. Steamers passing through must proceed very slowly, the larger ones having to be towed.

Many yachts approaching from the west find it convenient to visit the Ionian Islands first and then enter the Aegean by this route. (See under *Pilotage*.)

Though originally it was feared that there might be an inconvenient current, there is, in fact, seldom any flow of consequence, and only on rare occasions does it reach 2 knots due to strong winds. The sides of the Canal are continually breaking away and have to be repaired; this operation, which is performed on Sundays, involves closing the Canal, vessels being advised by 'loud hailer' as they approach the entrance.

Early History. This waterway was not cut until the 'eighties of the last century. The project was, however, seriously considered by both Caligula and Nero; the latter ordered a survey, and appeared in person to inaugurate the digging, lifting the first clod of earth with a golden shovel. The troublesome times which followed caused the undertaking to be abandoned, and thus the custom of hauling the galleys across the isthmus 'on rollers' continued through-out the centuries. The serious need for a canal did not again arise until the Austro-Lloyd Steamship Company secured the monopoly of the Levant trade during the last century. They found it necessary, though inconvenient, to build a good carriage road across the isthmus to convey their passengers arriving by sea at Loutraki to the steamer awaiting them at the other side.

> . . . *Salamis — where fame*
> *In noontide splendour shone,*
> *and blazed on Greece the deathless name*
> *That dawn'd at Marathon.*
>
> CARLYLE

Salamis is a hilly, arid island with a few clusters of trees and partial cultivation where there are small villages. Its interest to a yacht lies in the winding channels at either end (chart 1513) and the partly sheltered anchorages used mainly by Piraeus yachts when out for a day's sail.

At the eastern end lies the strait where the decisive battle took place in 492 B.C. The ledge where Xerxes is said to have sat watching the destruction of his 2,100 galleys by the 480 vessels of Themistocles' fleet is marked on the chart.

Cape Konkhi is an unusual and intriguing summer anchorage suitable only for a yacht drawing less than 8 feet. It lies among some rocky islets, and is comparatively well sheltered being open only to the west. It affords a splendid view of all the shipping passing to and fro between Piraeus and the Corinth Canal, and is pleasantly remote.

> **Approach and Anchorage.** On closing the lighthouse on the Cape turn eastwards keeping between the small islet and the shore. Though the depths shoal to 9 feet, it soon deepens again to 3 fathoms, as one approaches the anchorage where the sandy bottom continues.

Piraeus. There are two yacht harbours as well as the large commercial port—and a further yacht harbour 10 miles southwards on the Attic coast.

The Harbours of Passalimani (Zea) and Tourkolimano (Munychia), may be approached by day or night with the aid of Chart 1520.

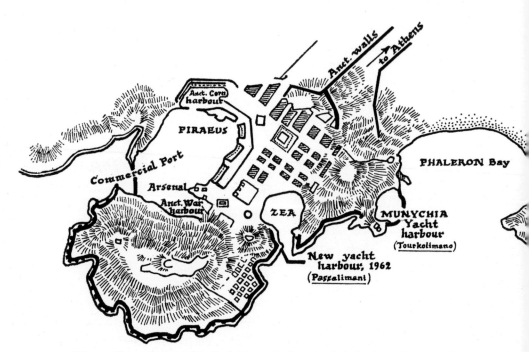

Piraeus, Zea and Munychia. Early Greek harbours and their adaptation to modern use

(a) **Passalimani.** In 1961 considerable improvements were being made here by the construction of a long breakwater* southward of the entrance and extending from the western shore. Dredging operations are intended to give the inner harbour depths of $2\frac{1}{4}$ fathoms and the new outer port $2\frac{1}{2}$ to 4 fathoms. The government has decreed it shall now revert to its former name of Zea.

(b) **Tourkolimano.** The depths here have recently been increased by dredging out the soft mud but the bottom is uneven. It has been difficult to find a berth in this congested harbour which, for its situation and the proximity of the Royal Hellenic Yacht Club, is the more desirable of the two harbours. One must obtain permission to berth here from the Secretary of the Yacht Club. The harbour is now to be called by its old name of Munychia.

Berthing in these harbours requires an anchor laid out ahead, and stern warps taken to a quay or to one or more yacht buoys. Both harbours can be smelly, and are very hot in summer.

Though laying-up afloat here for the winter months is practicable, southerly gales cause an uncomfortable swell inside. The new breakwater at Passalimani should obviate this drawback to a large extent.

Port Officials. Both Passalimani and Tourkolimano have a harbour authority to deal with Ship's Papers. Customs, Immigration and Police are at the commercial port of Piraeus, and are interested in foreign yachts; their representatives usually call to examine ship's papers.

Yacht Clubs. The Royal Hellenic Yacht Club, a palatial white building on the spur of the hill above Tourkolimano, is most helpful in advising visiting yachts.

The Piraeus Yacht Club situated on the shore beneath the R.H.Y.C. holds races for Star boats and dinghies, and can sometimes undertake minor repairs.

Port Facilities. Everything can be bought at Piraeus, especially close to Tourkolimano; there are yacht chandlers (expensive), restaurants and good provision shops (also expensive) close by the quays. Fuel, petrol and diesel, is to be obtained nearby. The best and cheapest chandlers are on the waterfront at Piraeus; here also is an excellent market. (Trolley-bus from Tourkolimano.)

Slipping and Repairs. Docking on skid-cradles can be undertaken at Perama, 3 miles west of Piraeus. The yard of George Psaros is often used by yachts, but is expensive; also Colourkari whose charges are more moderate.

Yacht stores may be sent out from England, but the procedure is only practical if the stores are sent out by sea and the yacht is in Piraeus to receive them. Many British stores, including paints and cordage, may be obtained in Athens at a cost of about 80% more than in England. A recommended customs agent for stores is Gerasimos Tsakalos, Nikita 2, Piraeus.

All around Tourkolimano are expensive restaurants with tables down to the water's edge, and every night throughout the summer months the place is tightly packed with diners, mostly Athenians, under glaring lamps enjoying

* With the completion of the new breakwater at the end of 1962, this harbour can now accommodate 300 yachts. The most convenient and sheltered berths are by the root of this long breakwater. Water, fuel and electricity are to be made available; harbour dues are charged on the basis of 100 drachmas per ton for a year.

their food in the cool of the evening. The harbour is crowded with yachts of every description.

Athens can be reached by taking a trolley-bus to Neo Phaleron Station whence the electric trains (every 6 minutes) reach Omonia Square in 20 minutes or Monasteraki in 15. Buses (every 15 minutes) reach Syntagma or Constitution Square in 35 minutes. Alternatively, buses run from the Demotic Theatre, Piraeus, and the electric trains from the Terminus station. A taxi costs about 15 shillings and takes 20 minutes.

The guide-book gives details of all that is of interest in Athens. No one should miss seeing at least the Acropolis and the National Museum. (All museums are closed on Mondays, and are free on Thursdays and Sundays.)

There is air and train communication with England: the aircraft in $3\frac{1}{2}$ hours and Direct Orient Express in 3 days. Local Greek airlines fly to Salonika, Mitylene, Rhodes, Kos, Crete, Kalamata and Corfu.

Brief History of the Harbours. The two yacht harbours were originally laid out in 493 B.C. when, in consequence of the Persian danger, Themistocles persuaded the Athenians to build stone breakwaters. These were largely of 10-foot square stone blocks on rubble foundations fastened with iron cramps run in with molten lead. The harbour approaches were then fortified and the two long walls leading to Athens were provided with adequate protection against enemy attack. Throughout the Venetian era the commercial harbour of Piraeus was generally known as Porto Leone, and although the marble lion was removed to Venice by Morosini in 1687, the port continued to be known by this name for at least another century. The lion now resides outside the Arsenal at Venice.

Vouliagmeni, 10 miles down the coast, a new yacht port, constructed in 1960–61, should be a welcome addition to the inadequate accommodation at Piraeus, as well as being suitable for laying-up. A fast road connects it with Athens.*

Approach. Chart 1657. The new breakwater may be seen extending from the small island across an underwater rock to the shore. The entrance is between a rock awash off the mole-head and the smaller of two islets.

Yachts berth stern to the quay in 3 fathoms: the shelter is all-round.

Facilities. Fresh water and fuel installations were in preparation (1961). The small village, a mile distant, has a few shops; from here, during the summer, buses run frequently to Athens.

The bay has been a popular bathing resort for many years.

* By the end of 1962 the harbour was completed with yacht facilities including a supply of water, fuel, electricity, and also a telephone on the quay. Judged to be safe in all weathers, this little port is administered by the Royal Hellenic Yacht Club (to whom dues are payable) and has been made a Port of Entry.

PART II: PIRAEUS TO SALONIKA

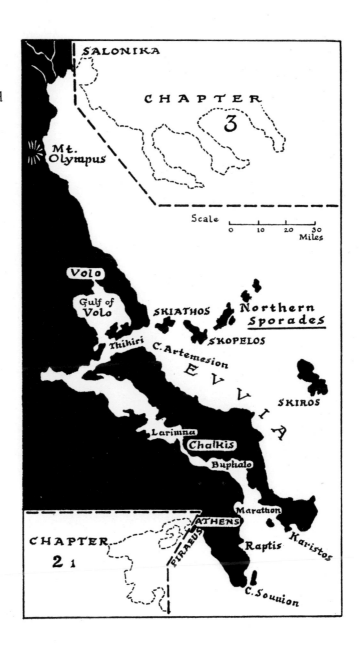

PART II: *PIRAEUS TO SALONIKA*

GULF OF ATHENS

Leaving Piraeus and sailing out of the Gulf of Athens (Saronic Gulf) there are some large sandy bays along the shores of the Attic coast. Though open in the southerly quadrant, they are all sheltered from the prevailing N.W. wind, and are much used as summer bathing resorts by Athenians, as well as being visited by yachts.

Vouliagmeni, about 9 miles from Athens by road, has been described at the end of the preceding chapter. There are many more bays including Port St Nicolo before reaching Sounion.

If passing between Gaidero Island and the Attic coast—a narrow though interesting passage—caution should be observed on account of the violent gusts from the hills during the afternoon in Meltemi conditions. All local craft have been observed to hand their sails.

> *Here in the dead of night by Lonna★ steep*
> *The seaman's cry was heard along the deep*
> FALCONER—after his shipwreck in *Britannia* on
> this Cape in 1762. He was one of the three saved.

Sounion. One can see Cape Sounion in the distance and, against the blue sky, the temple of Poseidon whose columns of Attic marble now appear quite white, and are in fact crystallized and glazed with the salt spray of twenty-four centuries. To the early Greek seamen this headland with its historic temple was the last they saw of their mother country as they sailed out to the Ionian colonies and the distant domains that were once the glory of the Greek Empire.

'Place me on Sounion's marbled steep', wrote Byron; and here the poet, in common with many others, has chiselled his name at the base of one of the columns.

The view from the cape is magnificent. In the north are the peaks of Hymettus—'the happy hunting ground of bees'—and sweeping towards the west lie the islands of Aegina, Poros and Hydra; further to the south and the east can be seen the dark silhouettes of the mountainous Cyclades with Kithnos and Kea, and the nearby Makronisos.

★ Lonna, a corruption of Colonna, the Venetian name for Sounion.

'A range of columns long by time defaced'

Anchorage presents no difficulties, there being depths of 2 to 3 fathoms on a sea bed of sand, stones and weed within 70 yards of the sandy beach. This bay is much visited by yachts during the summer, and being open only to south there is normally smooth water. A short stone pier makes a convenient landing-place for the dinghy.

Nearby are some recently opened expensive restaurants, and a motel which somewhat mars the beauty of the temple on the skyline.

THE TWO ROUTES NORTHWARD FROM THE GULF OF ATHENS

If leaving the Gulf and being northward bound, a decision must be reached whether to pass inside the narrow channel between the long mountainous island of Evvia and the Attic–Beoetian coast, or make the northing in the open waters of the Aegean.

Evvia with its tall rugged mountains, fertile plains, forests and mines is, after Crete, the largest island in the Aegean. During recent years it has been known as Negropont (Venetian), Euboea (Greek), Evvoia, and Evvia (transcription of Euboea).

37

It has two principal ports: Chalkis in the narrow Euripo Strait (described later) and Karistos lying in a bay the southern end of the island. This small town standing beneath Mount Ochi has an artificial port for small vessels; it was from here that much of the marble was shipped to Rome. Yet a third but smaller port, Kimi, lies on the east coast; this is protected by two breakwaters and is the supply port for the island of Skiros, and much used by caiques as well as being a port of call for the mail steamers.

THE OPEN-WATER ROUTE

Until after the First World War when caiques still had no motors, they always chose the open-water route* to make their northing. When bound for Salonika they took advantage of the fact that the N.W. wind blowing from the Attic shores in the summer, changes its direction as one moves farther eastward. Thus sailing vessels, having stood across, were often favoured with an easterly slant enabling them to fetch right up the Salonika Gulf.

The open-water route takes a sailing vessel to the north-eastward, passing through the Kea and Doro channels, where anchorages on Andros Island are described in Chapter 6.

> **Pilotage Notes on Route.** The currents in these channels especially Doro Channel, occasionally run to the southward very fast during fresh northerly winds—as much as 5 or 6 knots. If desiring to await better conditions, there is good anchorage in Gavrion Bay in Andros, and there are two sheltered bays on the opposite shore of Evvia:
> (*a*) Kastri Bay, with good holding on firm sand in 3 fathoms.
> (*b*) A bay unnamed 1¼ miles N.E. of Kastri.
> Both bays (with fresh-water springs) afford good shelter from the Meltemi.

THE INNER PASSAGE BETWEEN EVVIA AND THE MAINLAND
(*Gulfs of Petali and Evvia*)

During the summer months, this is often a long haul to windward. Passing by the Petali Gulf to Chalkis and thence the Gulf of Evvia, altogether 76 miles, the passage leads between the narrow island of Makronisi (a prohibited landing place) and the Attic shore. There are the bays of Mandri and Ergesteria or Lavrion (an ore port) which are suitable for temporary shelter, but of no interest to a yacht. Working up this coast, the first place worthy of a call is:

---

* A similar choice was made by Odysseus when returning from Troy. 'In this dilemma we prayed for a sign, and heaven made it clear that we should cut straight across the open sea to Eubea'.

Port Raptis, 15 miles from Sounion, a charming anchorage in the green hilly surroundings of the Attic coast.

Approach. Chart 1526. On the small but steep island, which forms the protection for the bay, stands a marble statue of a headless tailor, from which the place takes its name. This is a splendid seamark and enables one to identify the port.

The anchorage, with convenient depths on a clear sandy bottom, is off the small hamlet of St Spyridon close offshore by some trees. It is open to east and S.E., and though some swell may come in, the wind does not blow home.

Facilities. There are one or two tavernas (where a meal may be had), fresh provision shops, and general stores. In the summer months, buses run frequently to Athens in about an hour.

This little port, which now has a loading quay for caiques in the S.W. corner, appears to be increasing in importance. A number of villas have been built on the slopes near the hamlet.

Early History. The origin of the headless statue is obscure. It appears at first sight to belong to the sixth century B.C.; but it is also said to be of Roman origin. It is believed that during the period of the Confederation the annual ceremony of transporting the Thoria to Holy Delos took place here. In later centuries when sailing vessels from the west used these waters, the shelter of Raptis was well known: John Sellers states in *Sailing Directions* of 24 July 1677 'Port Raptis is one of the best and most commodious havens of all that are found in the archipelago to sail into in stress of weather'.

The **Petali Islands** consist of a small group lying towards Evvia on the east side of the gulf. The sheltered anchorage between Megalo and Xero islands (in 5 fathoms near a large white house) is sometimes useful to a yacht wishing to put in for the night. There are no amenities, and the attraction of the coastal features has recently been spoilt by the presence of some laid-up shipping.

> *That man is little to be envied whose patriotism*
> *would not gain force upon the Plain of Marathon.*
> DR JOHNSON

Marathon is a large bay mainly of interest for its historical associations. The best anchorage for a yacht is off some small houses in the pinewood in the northern corner of the bay. Here are convenient depths, and the peninsula projecting southwards affords good protection except in southerly winds. The modern summer village on the N.W. wide of the bay usually has a few boats moored off, but this place is too exposed to the afternoon breeze.

Early History. Behind the 'Dog's Tail' (Cynosura) lies the anchorage of the Persian fleet, and where the pinewoods now grow, the site of the evacuation of the Persian army. It was here in 490 B.C. that the Athenians drove them back to their galleys drawn up on this beach. The famous tumulus where 192 Athenians lie buried has been tidied up, and there are now trees and gardens as well as a small pavilion for tourists.

A better place to anchor for the night is at Buphalo, distant only 12 miles from Marathon on the Evvia coast. This is a charming sheltered little cove at the head of a small creek with only half a dozen cottages and some small fishing craft.

Buphalo

Approach and Anchorage. Chart 2802. There is deep water everywhere except near the projecting sand spit from the eastern shore. Anchor in the middle of the small basin in 3½ fathoms on firm sand. Here there is nearly all-round shelter and sufficient room to swing.

Along the coast is grazing country and a few cornfields.

Aliverion. If in need of a proper port with a village, Aliverion is easily recognized by an Hellenic tower and Venetian castle. A yacht should round the mole-head (Chart 1597) and berth stern to a quay by the village. This little place has been dwarfed by the nearby Pyrgos where a huge power plant has been built.

So they passed by Crouni and Chalkis a land of fair streams
ODYSSEY XV

Chalkis is a pleasant, modernized town with a rickety swing bridge connecting the island of Evvia with the mainland. The narrow winding channels through which a vessel from the south approaches the place are interesting both from the pilotage point of view as well as the scenery: the fortress, defended towers, and campanile are all Venetian.

Chalkis—looking southward, showing where Northbound traffic should anchor to await opening of swing-bridge

Typical rigs of Aegean craft no longer to be seen. Though these rigs have all vanished the classical hull continues under power and a small gaff-mainsail has been introduced as a steadying sail.

A large Sacoulevi with Barkalas hull, formerly built in Samos and Sira.

Barkalas hull, Black Sea rig (mast or yard sometimes in tabernacle)

Bratsera, Trehanderi hull
Sacoulevi, Perama hull

At the narrowest part by the bridge, the tidal streams run swiftly, changing direction about every 6 hours, but considerably influenced by wind and barometer. The stream can occasionally run as fast as 8 knots and it begins almost immediately after the turn of the tide. The traffic, controlled by signal from the control tower by the bridge, must pass *with* the stream: only warships and mail-boats may proceed either with or against it as they desire.

The Byzantine church of Paraskevi in the old town should be visited; also the old Turkish mosque and fountain.

Approach. Chart 2802. There is no difficulty, even in a hard Meltemi, in beating through the narrow channels leading northwards towards the Bridge.

Berth. (*a*) *South of Bridge.* It is recommended to anchor close off the projecting quay by the railway station. This is out of the tide and sheltered: landing by dinghy it is only 2 minutes' walk to the control office which directs the opening of the bridge. Here one must pay the small fee for passing through, and enquire about the next opening. (Normally it is at the turn of the tide, so that small vessels, which have been waiting, may all pass through *with* the tide.)

(*b*) *North of the Bridge.* Anchor near the bridge, off the western shore by the local Lido. This is about 20 yards N.W. of the southernmost mooring buoy, where the depth is about 3 fathoms. It is out of the strong tide and reasonably sheltered even in a northerly blow.

Port Facilities. The quays on the eastern side of the channel, south of the bridge, accommodate small steamers, and a yacht can find a temporary berth here if desired. Diesel fuel and fresh water are sometimes available, but cannot be depended upon.

There is an excellent market. The recently built modern hotel, some good restaurants and shops have given Chalkis a new and thriving look. A train service connects with Athens in 2 hours. There is also a bus, and the mail-boat from Piraeus calls.

After leaving Chalkis and entering the **Gulf of Evvia** the scenery now becomes more attractive and the mountains reach their greatest height—nearly 6,000 feet of limestone cliff—standing almost sheer above the green coastline. A sailing yacht must keep towards the mainland shore, as the mountain squalls can be hard; moreover the anchorages are all on the Beoetian coast of the mainland.

Larimna, the present name of the ancient port of Larmes, lies 16 miles N.W. of Chalkis, at the mouth of the River Caphissus. Off the small village are convenient depths for anchoring, but the interesting approach is somewhat marred by the derelict buildings of an ore company.

The ancient river still flows and provides cooling water for a bathe at the anchorage; formerly running underground, it was used to drive the mills of the early Greeks, and shafts were sunk to enable men to descend and prevent blocking. Some of these shafts may still be seen.

E—T.A.

Atalanta Channel is approached farther to the north-west, and then leads southwards.

Anchorages. (*a*) In Atalanta Channel, off a small jetty with a road leading to Atalanta village standing on a hill 3 miles distant.

(*b*) Farther south at Port Armyro where there is a seldom-used ore pier.

(Both these pleasant and remote anchorages may be studied on Chart 1556, and local instructions for the approach appear in *Sailing Directions*.)

At the end of Evvia Gulf and 42 miles above the swing-bridge of Chalkis, are the islands of Likhadhes with passages leading into the Oreos Gulf to the N.E., and the Maliakos Gulf to the west. The narrow N.E. passage (250 yards wide) between Evvia and the island is quite practical by day; though here the tidal stream can run at 3 knots (in the main channel it is about half this velocity).

Though the mail-boat was wrecked on the sandy spit a few years ago one should not be discouraged from making this inshore passage; it is necessary to pass well within 100 yards of the point to avoid underwater rocks on the western side of the fairway.

GULF OF OREOS

It is not proposed to describe the western or Maliakos Gulf which leads to the ore and bauxite loading quays at Stilis with the pass of Thermopylae beyond. This gulf has no appeal.

Turning eastwards, the Oreos Gulf separating Evvia from the Thessaly coast leads past the entrance to the Gulf of Volo towards the attractive islands of the Northern Sporades. Every afternoon in summer the N.E. breeze blows freshly down the gulf and whips up a short steep sea.

Anchorage. There are one or two anchorages in the gulf: one behind a short mole off Oreos village—a dull little place but well sheltered against the day breeze: another, more interesting though less safe, is on the opposite shore:

Trikiri, an open bay with a primitive hamlet standing at the foot of the mountain, guards the approach to the Gulf of Volo.

Approach and Berth. There is no difficulty by day for the water is very deep and the village is conspicuous. On account of the sea-bed rising too steeply to permit anchoring off, a vessel must proceed to the N.E. corner of the bay, letting go in 10 fathoms and hauling in the stern to a small stone pier. There are a couple of mooring buoys close off whose ground cables should be avoided.

Historical. A spirited action took place in this little bay during the Greek War of Independence. On 23 April 1827 Captain Abney Hastings, then fighting for Greece, was commanding one of the earliest aux-steam gunboats, named *Karteria*. This 4-masted vessel was built of iron, with tall thin funnel, fore and aft rig with square topsails, and also driven by paddles. She had already harassed the ships of the Turkish Navy then blockading the Greek coast off Volo, and on this occasion her opponent was a large Turkish brig moored close to the shore and protected by a battery on the hill above.

She was sighted by *Karteria* who, approaching from seaward, immediately prepared for action. Driven by her 40 horse-power engines she rapidly closed the enemy. Meanwhile in the boilers—each 23 feet long—cannon shot was being heated and when within range Hastings opened fire. The red-hot shot soon had the brig alight and in an hour she was completely burnt out. Hastings has not been forgotten by the Greeks, for his statue stands in a prominent position in the Garden of Heroes at Messolongion.

Volo is a large gulf, now styled 'Pargasitikos', with a busy modern town at its head. Though the port is clean and sheltered, it is seldom that a yacht makes this long detour for a special visit.

Approach and Berth. Chart 1196. The entrance is straight-forward day or night. Yachts and coasters usually berth stern to the quay, near the centre of the town, where the bottom is soft mud. In the summer months the afternoon breeze is usually from the southward.

Port Facilities. Good water is available from a hydrant at the root of the mole, and a hose is provided. Diesel fuel and petrol can be bought and ordinary repairs undertaken. Taxis are also available. Some modern hotels have recently been built and there are one or two good restaurants on the front.

Frequent diesel trains run to Larissa—on the main line.

Steamer communication with Piraeus and the northern ports.

Officials. As necessary for a Port of Entry.

Volo has developed considerably in the last 25 years and is now the fourth largest town of Greece. It suffered early in 1955 from a severe earthquake when a number of the older buildings were destroyed, but prompt action by the authorities soon restored the town to working order.

The country round Volo, both on Mt Pelion itself and on the coast beneath it, is attractive. To avoid the heat of Volo in the summer evenings, a drive to Portaria (half way up Pelion) is recommended; there is a small hotel with a good restaurant and a terrace with enormous plane trees. Along the coast there are little villages among olive groves where one may also dine simply, but well.

Cape Artemesion. Continuing eastwards out of the Trikiri Strait towards the Sporades one passes the N.E. headland of Evvia, Cape Artemesion, where in 480 B.C. 100 Athenian warships, together with some allied vessels, had their first engagement with the invading Persian fleet.

Historical. Only a couple of years ago, with the discovery of a white marble slab at Troezen, details came to light of the naval strategy employed by Themistocles to save Athens from the coming Persian invasion. The writing on the slab explains the employment of delaying tactics to be adopted by the Athenian warships off Cape Artemesion: it directs that the triremes' crews should consist of a captain, 20 marines and 4 archers; and it gives the disposition of the other 100 triremes which were to lie off Salamis and the Attic coast to 'keep guard over the land'. Before these details were revealed, it was never realized that Themistocles had carefully planned the Battle of Salamis.

NORTHERN SPORADES

Including Skyros there are nine islands, some of which are of great interest and beauty.

Skiathos, lying nearest to the Oreos channel, is low-lying and thickly wooded. The harbour has good natural protection and there is an attractive little town standing on two hills close beside it. This was built early in the last century

Volo Gulf, and Oreos Channel and northern Sporades

after the abolition of piracy, and has now eclipsed in importance the early capital Kastro, perched on a rocky spur on the other side of the island. The island's population is about 4,000.

Approach. Chart 1196. There is good anchorage in 3 fathoms behind the small wooded island off the caique quay in the North Harbour. The bottom is thin weed on marl and the depths shoal rapidly close to the quay.
Facilities. There is a fresh-water tap by the quay. Petrol may be bought at a B.P. station. There are two or three restaurants on the waterfront where the food is good and lobsters are often available. Simple provisions are to be obtained.

General. Apart from a statue to the local Greek writer Papadiamandis, the only other thing of interest is the local shipyard. Although there is nothing particular to offer at Skiathos, it has much charm, and the gardens of the little houses grow an abundance of flowers.

The Aegean's best bathing beach Koukunarias (meaning stone-pines) lies only a few miles to the westward and affords convenient anchorage in calm weather.

Skopelos, an equally green island, is also rocky with sharply defined mountain ridges. Some of the wooded valleys lead steeply upwards to attractive monasteries still inhabited by monks.

There are two ports and a few sheltered coves: Glossa, opposite Skiathos, has not only the best natural shelter, but on its tall slopes grows the most luxuriant vegetation with masses of fruit trees (including plums, an island speciality) and olives. (Glossa is marked 'Klima' on the Admiralty chart.)

Skopelos, the capital, on the other side of the island, is unfortunate in having an artificial port so exposed to N.E. gales that sometimes it becomes quite unusable. It lies in a lovely setting, with the houses of the town, (many colour-washed in shades of yellow and pink, with their gables picked out in white), rising like the sides of an amphitheatre almost overshadowing the port. Above are olive groves; here and there clusters of cypresses, and vineyards beyond.

Port Skopelos

Approach. *Sailing Directions* explain position of breakwaters. In 1960 the end of the outer mole had been destroyed and its extremity marked by an insignificant beacon. There were no lights. The depth at the entrance is 3 fathoms.

Berth. Steer for a position the eastern side of the village by a square with tavernas on the waterfront. Here there are depths of 9 feet, and a yacht may berth stern to the quay, bows northward. Both moles are built with rough ballasting and there is shallow water close off and also in the vicinity of the short stone pier. It would be unwise to enter here in a northerly blow and uncomfortable to remain here during a strong Meltemi.

Port Facilities. There are one or two good fresh provision shops, and ice may be bought. A simple restaurant and one or two tavernas are close by. Good fresh water may be obtained by hose from a locked tap on the quay, but it is necessary to bargain first about the price.

The island has half a dozen monasteries in the hills. Two, high above the port, still inhabited amidst charming scenery form the objective for some delightful walks. There is a bus service to Glossa.

Suitable anchorage may be found on the southern shore at Staphilis Bay and at Agonia in the event of the Meltemi making entry into Port Skopelos too hazardous.

45

Pelagos is an uninhabited wooded island (1,300 feet) with a delightfully green mountainous anchorage and all-round shelter at

Port Planedhi

Approach and Anchorage. Chart 2072. There is no difficulty by day, and *Sailing Directions* give a good description. Though the channel is only 90 yards wide at its narrowest point, there need be no difficulty in beating through.

The S.E. arm of the harbour is the most suitable anchorage; here the bottom is firm mud, and shelter is complete.

Except for a small monastery a little way inland, there are no permanent inhabitants on this island. A couple of caiques call here in summer to load charcoal which is prepared close to the shore and then shipped to Salonika.

Despite the fact that the anchorage is entirely enclosed by high mountains, it is refreshingly cool and there is a potent smell of herbs.

Peristera is a barren uninhabited island having some small inlets at its southern end. The principal bay is known as **Port Vasiliko.** It is almost land-locked and except for a couple of cottages there is no sign of life.

Approach and Anchorage. Chart 2072. Passing between Alonnisos and Peristera, a yacht should anchor in 5 fathoms at the head of the bay, running a warp to the western shore if necessary. The shelter is almost all-round and only in the event of a S.W. wind could a fetch of 2 miles cause some inconvenience.

Alonnisos. A cove, lying 3½ miles N.E. of Cape Notos, affords suitable night anchorage, and in summer is used as such by fishing craft. A village approached by a track lies on the hill above and is one hour's walk.

Skyros or **Skiros,** is a rugged mountainous island partly wooded with a village of the same name lying inland on the shoulder of the tall mountain. There are two main harbours:

(*a*) **Linaria Cove** is well sheltered in an attractive setting; it is the main port for Skyros and has an adjoining hamlet.

Approach and Berth. Chart 2048. Though there is no difficulty by day, at night the passage north of Valexa Island could be difficult. Though the light is unreliable, the white house above it is conspicuous.

Anchor as near as one prudently can towards the S.E. corner of the bay. The bottom is clay or mud, but it rises sharply from a considerable depth, and care is necessary to find a convenient sea bed at 3 or 4 fathoms at the same time clear of the caiques.

The new quay can be of use to a yacht drawing a maximum of 8 feet, provided no ferries want to berth here.

Facilities. There is a water tap by the nearer taverna: petrol and diesel oil may be bought. Provisions are almost unobtainable—bread can be bought, however. Ice arrives on alternate days by caique from Evvia. There are two tavernas, and a small modern hotel has recently been built.

The Piraeus steamer calls weekly, and a large caique from Kymi calls on alternate days, bringing passengers and mail.

The village of Skyros with its acropolis at the east side of the island is worth a visit, and may be reached by bus in 20 minutes. There is a simple but good restaurant and a few provision shops; also a small museum of local finds.

The statue of Rupert Brooke stands in an imposing position north of Skyros village looking across the brilliantly coloured sand and over water of many shades of blue towards the distant Aegean islands beyond. Brooke died on board a French hospital ship when on the point of sailing for Gallipoli early in 1915. Winston Churchill, writing to *The Times* on 26 April, said, 'A voice had become audible, a note had been struck, more true, more thrilling, more able to do justice to the nobility of our youth in arms engaged in the present war than any other . . . The voice has been swiftly stilled'.

(*b*) **Port Trebuki** (Tres Boukes). The southern anchorage is more suitable for large vessels than for yachts, and though a yacht may tuck into one of the creeks, strong gusts from the mountains spoil the tranquillity of the place. The main interest here is the grave of Rupert Brooke which is a few minutes' walk from the head of one of these creeks.

Mythological Note on Skyros. It was here that Thetis decided to protect the young Achilles by disguising him as a maiden among the daughters of Lycomedes. 'What songs the Syrens sang, or what name Achilles assumed when he hid himself among the women' wrote the witty seventeenth-century writer Sir Thomas Browne 'though puzzling questions, are not beyond all conjecture'.

The bones of Theseus were also found on the island, and according to Thucydides were then conveyed to Athens to be enshrined in the Theseum.

THE COAST FROM THE NORTHERN SPORADES TO SALONIKA

This coast is straight and without shelter for 100 miles. The predominating feature is Mt Olympus, nearly ten thousand feet, and the high mountains in the vicinity.

The Thermai Gulf leads into the Gulf of Salonika and, though there are some possible night anchorages close off the coast, they are completely open and practical only in flat calm weather.

The Meltemi can blow in strength from the Axios River (formerly the Vardar, and renowned for the duck shooting) down the Gulf. This happens for periods of only 2 or 3 days, often followed by a S.W. sea breeze blowing up the Gulf every afternoon.

NORTHERN SHORES OF THE AEGEAN

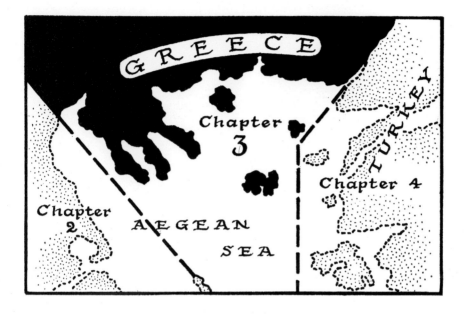

This chapter covers the seaboard of Grecian Macedonia
and Thrace to the Turkish frontier.

Salonika
Ascent of Mt Olympus
Chalkidhiki Peninsula
Port Koupho
Sikias Bay
Port Dimitri
Head of the Singitic Gulf
Ammouliani Island
Holy Mountain

Daphne
Vatopedi Bay
Kavalla
Thasos
Alexandroupolis
Samothrace
Limnos
Kastro
Evstratios

3

Northern Shores of the Aegean

The western part of this coast, especially the Chalcydice Peninsula and the island of Thasos, is of great beauty. Here, the summer winds blow with considerably less strength than in the southern Aegean.

Salonika, the second city of Greece with a large commercial port, has been the capital of Macedonia since earliest times. Unfortunately it lacks yacht berthing facilities.

Approach and Berth. Chart 2070. There is no difficulty day or night in reaching the harbour, but berthing presents a problem.

There appear to be only two alternatives and both are near the Harbour Master's office (*a*) near Customs, but N.W. side of east mole; or (*b*) S.E. side of east mole, which during the Meltemi is well sheltered.

It is also possible to berth off the Yacht Club, but this is rather exposed and smelly, as well as being far from where one wants to shop in the town. Off the water-front where the larger ferry-boats berth is uncomfortable for a yacht on account of the disturbed sea caused by the afternoon breeze.

Officials. This is a Port of Entry. Customs, Immigration, Health and Port Authority.

General. Everything can be bought within 10 minutes of the port. Fresh water is laid on at the quays. There are many restaurants large and small. A British Consulate-General is established across the main square, and here are also ship chandlers. Nearby is a very good market where most things can be found, including an abundance of Macedonian fruit.

Salonika is connected with Athens by air (2 hours) and by train (12 hours). By Tauern Express to London takes 2½ days.

Officially known by its ancient name of Thessaloniki, it presents a great contrast to the walled oriental town captured from the Turks in 1912. The large cemeteries outside the town are evidence of its occupation by Allied troops during World War I. Between the two wars some progress was made in rebuilding, but in 1940 with the German invasion the place sank to a low ebb. However, all these misfortunes have now been forgotten and one sees the bold façade of a modern and prosperous-looking city with esplanades, public squares, large hotels and skyscrapers.

The guide-book describes the town's associations since the days of St Paul, and the historic Byzantine churches, which together with the ramparts and the White Tower should be visited.

> *. . . yet here will I*
> *Upon Olympus' lofty ridge remain,*
> *And view, serene, the combat;*
>
> ILIAD XX

Climbing. Advice on climbing Mount Olympus can be obtained at Salonika from the Greek Alpine Club. It is advisable to have a guide. The starting base is Litochoron, nearly two hours by train towards Athens, and the expedition takes about 3 days. Given fine weather it is well worth undertaking, most of the ascent being gentle, through wooded country; only the last 800 feet can be called a 'scramble'.

From Litochoron the lofty peak of Mitika rising to nearly 10,000 feet is often visible about 10 miles away.

Near the village mules may be hired to carry blankets and provisions. It is advisable to make a start early in the forenoon in order to reach the first camp comfortably by dusk. A goat-track threading its way through pinewoods and evergreens slowly gains height as it eventually joins a running stream.

Towards the end of the day one should arrive at a protruding ridge at an altitude of 6,800 feet, and here is the place to camp. Known to the Greeks as 'The Grotto', the site is well sheltered, lying between a rock-face and the edge of the forest. Though the temperature falls rapidly at this level, one may spend a comfortable night close to a wood fire, sleeping on a pine-needle bed.

To reach the summit the following day it is necessary to start before dawn, at the same time sending the mules with blankets and remaining provisions to a monastery on the other face of the mountain, lying on the route of the intended descent.

For a couple of hours, one must make through open country where partridges abound and eagles, wild goat and boar are to be seen. If one is lucky, an inspiring view may be had of the sun rising close behind Mt Athos nearly 100 miles away. At 9,000 feet one reaches an easy knife-edge and a small cairn called Brigand's Tower.

This is where the scramble begins—a steep-sided Punchbowl with loose shale all round and nothing to hold on to. (For one's feet, gym shoes are as good as anything.) Progress must now be slow, and care is needed not to dislodge the loose stones upon those beneath; though a rope is sometimes used, it is of little advantage.

The summit, a small pinnacle with barely space for ten people should be reached by midday. The view on a clear day is magnificent—the Balkan ranges rolling away to the north, Athos to the east, Parnassus to the south with Pelion and Ossa rather nearer to the south-west.

The first 800 feet of the descent, unfortunately can be made only by the same insecure route, and the shelter of the monastery must be reached by dusk where the mules with blankets and provisions should have arrived. The final descent by mule-track should be made the following morning—i.e. on the third day.

THE COAST FROM SALONIKA—EASTWARDS

The Chalkidhiki Peninsula on the chart appears like a folded hand with three fingers sticking out into the Aegean. These are the peninsulas of Kassandra, Sithonia (sometimes called Sithonia Longos) and Athos. All are green and wooded, hilly or mountainous country.

Kassandra which is mainly pastoral and agricultural country, has a canal across its neck, which has been allowed to silt so much that in 1960 there was a depth of barely 7 feet. There are no suitable anchorages off the Kassandra shores, but 80 miles from Salonika and near the head of Sithonia is the beautiful land-locked harbour of

Port Koupho

Approach and Anchorage. Chart 1679. There is no difficulty day or night, for it is well lit. It is best to proceed to the top of Goras bay and anchor here off the hamlet in 4 fathoms, 70 yards off shore. The bottom is fine weed or mud, and the shelter is all round.

General. Close by are three or four little houses and a few farms. The setting here is lovely, with pine forests and olive groves. A short stone pier has recently been built and a church was under construction in 1960.

There are some interesting caverns in the hillside west of the anchorage.

Sikias Bay. Barely a dozen miles from Port Koupho, it lies close to the mouth of the Singitikos gulf—a pleasant deserted sandy bay, sheltered on three sides, and well worth a call.

>**Approach and Anchorage.** Chart 1679—inset. There is no difficulty day or night. The best anchorage is in 3 fathoms where indicated in the southern corner of bay. It is firm sand, and a perfect bathing beach. If it blows from the N.E. this anchorage is no longer comfortable.
>**General.** The hamlet of Sikia is 1½ miles inland, otherwise there is no connection with civilization.

Port Dimitri. Lying deeper in this Gulf is the lovely island of Dimitri providing land-locked coves between it and the mainland—here too the country is

Port Dimitri. (*Soundings in fathoms*)

hilly and green with clusters of poplars and cypresses near the shore merging into olive groves close behind; a background of dark green pinewoods rises to the skyline beyond.

>**Approach and Anchorage.** Chart 1679 and *Sailing Directions* imply that the entry is more formidable than it actually is. The plan should simplify this—at the northern entrance a beacon with a flashing light has been placed on the islet to S.W. of Peristeri. Except in very bright moonlight it would be unwise to approach either entrance by night.
>   Care is necessary when choosing an anchorage, for the bottom rises rather steeply, and a

flat sea bed is lacking, Shelter is all-round and there is sand, or weed on sand, at some of the anchorages.

There are only one or two small houses belonging to fishermen temporarily on the island; and on the mainland a number of farmhouses by a road connecting with Salonika.

Head of the Singitic Gulf. Across the gulf is the narrow isthmus of the Akti or Athos peninsula where Xerxes in 481 B.C. dug a canal to enable his galley fleet to pass in safety and avoid the much-feared storms off the headland. Landing at Tripita and walking inland, some of the diggings can still be discerned, and though the land here must still be about the same level above the sea as then, the sea bed close-by has sunk. In 12-fathom depths remains of sunken ships can be seen and also traces of early wharves.

Ammouliani Island. Lying a mile off the isthmus, this island has a small fishing population. Though indented and irregular in shape, it is unattractive and rather barren. Certain coves indicated on the chart afford useful anchorage to small vessels, according to the weather.

In the summer months there is daily communication with Salonika by caique which brings provisions and ice.

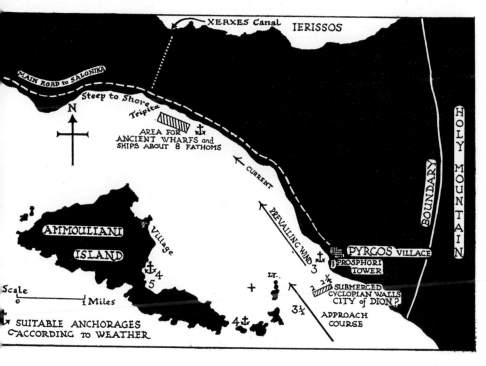

On the Peninsula towards the frontier of the Holy Mountain is the prominent seamark of Prosphori, an eighth-century tower. In contrast, the adjoining village of Pyrgos (which also means Tower) is very new, having been built to accommodate the Greek population deported from one of the Princes Islands, in the Sea of Marmara, after the First World War. They are very poor and the village is largely without water. The construction of a modern hotel for tourists in 1960 may perhaps benefit the villagers.

Close offshore a long reef on which the seas break heavily during storms extends more than 2 fathoms under water. The sea bed on the southern side of the reef falls away quickly and at one place the Cyclopean walls of some early construction, long since submerged, can still be clearly seen.

In fine weather it is convenient to anchor in 2½ fathoms 200 yards N.W. of the Tower.

THE HOLY MOUNTAIN (Akti Peninsula)

Less than a mile from the Tower is the frontier of the Holy Mountain with its dwindling population of little more than 2,000 monks, still leading a monastic life. There are altogether twenty monasteries, undoubtedly seen at their best

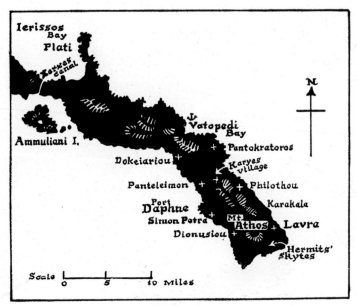

The Holy Mountain

The Corinth Canal

Thasos: harbour from the Acropolis

MONASTERIES AT ATHOS

Simon Petra

Dionysiou

from seaward and, therefore, a yacht which can stand in close when desired or go alongside a jetty is ideal for the occasion. Some monasteries were built at the time of Justinian in the sixth century A.D.; others at later periods. Most of them stand dramatically on various mountain spurs, or are tucked into the mouth of some green valley, or have grown up on fertile land close to the sea. With the exception of one or two relatively modern ones, each monastery is usually a heterogeneous cluster of Byzantine buildings in colourful shades of red or blue and conspicuous for their domes and cupolas. Though varying considerably in size and shape, when seen as one unit they nearly all look attractive in their green mountainous setting.

The Peninsula, which is nearly 25 miles long, is rugged and steep on its western side, whereas the eastern slopes are gentle and covered in a great variety of trees. Close to the ridge itself on both sides there is forestation—beech and chestnuts above, oaks and plane trees below—also a flowering undergrowth. The long ridge forming a backbone reaches its peak (Mt Athos) near the extremity of the peninsula where it rises to over 6,000 feet; here it is rather bare and stands abruptly out of the sea.

Daphne is the Control Port for the Holy Mountain—a temporary place of call if landing on the Athos Peninsula—and lies about half-way along the shores of the Singitic gulf.

A Customs Officer and Police are stationed here to examine papers and possessions of visitors to the Holy Mountain. Women may not land, and men intending to do so must have the Greek Foreign Office permit.

Approach and Berth. About 100 yards S.E. of a light-tower is a small quay with a stone pier, having a depth of 6 feet at its extremity. The sea bed rises sharply, and 70 yards off is a heavy mooring-buoy suitable for steamers; but near the pierhead is a patch of sand (which is not good holding) sufficient to hold off a yacht's bows when temporarily hauling her stern up to the end of the pier.

The prevailing wind does not blow home and though entirely open, one may expect sufficient shelter from the curvature of the coast during ordinary summer conditions.

General. There are one or two rather modest little shops, and a fresh water tap close by. The mule track leads to Karies, the principal village of Athos, where permits to land on the Holy Mountain are again examined.

Continuing along the shore one sees the striking monastery of Simon Peter built solidly into the cliff, reminiscent of those fortress-like structures in Tibet. Further towards the top of the peninsula, and standing on the steep mountainside appear small houses. They are in fact the abodes of hermits and occasionally a monk may be seen under the shade of his black umbrella climbing up to one of these solitary habitations; some, even more primitive, appear as mountain

F—T.A.

caves, and are accessible only by ladder; others seem to have no visible mode of access at all and cling to the steep cliff like swallows' nests.

The sea off the extremity of the Cape can be very disturbed, and under certain conditions violent squalls sweep down from the mountain slopes. Mardonius experienced a phenomenonal storm in 491 B.C. when from a clear sky a sudden Levanter blew up and wrecked the Persian invading fleet of 300 vessels.

Rounding the massive headland and approaching the north-eastern shores of the Peninsula you come to one of the oldest and most attractive of the monasteries, Lavra—here, one may land to climb the mountain; but the Lilliput harbour cut into the cliff close under the monastery can accommodate only the smallest caiques. Other monasteries have short piers where landing can be made in calm weather. There is only one good summer anchorage on the N.E. shore of the peninsula and this is beneath the large monastery of Vatopedi.

Vatopedi Bay

Approach and Anchorage. Steer for the monastery buildings and let go 100 yards off the small stone pier in 4 fathoms. Holding is good, but the bay is open to the northern quadrant.
General Information. A policeman is on duty at the quay to check the coming and going of visitors and local people who have no direct connection with the monasteries.

During part of the summer a few of the night fishing fleet are based here, but their catch seems to be meagre. The monastery still has its ancient aqueduct, and there is plenty of water available in the buildings today.

The only good shelter on this N.E. coast is at Plati, in Ierissos Bay; this is the most convenient base for making day excursions to those monasteries having small jetties. Unfortunately the holding at Plati is uncertain.

THE COAST FROM HOLY MOUNTAIN TO THASOS STRAIT

Passing Ierissos Bay and continuing northwards, you approach the mountainous wooded slopes at the head of the Gulf of Strimon. On the sandy shores lies the village of Stavros and behind it an extensive plain reaching to the foothills beyond.

The setting is appealing, though the anchorage off the pier by the village is exposed to the southerly swell. North of the village, the waters of the Rendina River flowing from Lake Volvi (or Beshik) enter the sea. The gorge is attractive and may be followed for 6 miles as far as the lake; it is also partly navigable by boat, though the stream can flow swiftly in places.

Ten miles N.E. a more important river, the Struma, exudes its muddy waters into the Aegean. Under the ancient name of Strymon in Greco-Roman days, it formed the artery for the port of Eion close to the city of Amphipolis sometimes visited by St Paul. Today there are a few remains, but by the road-bridge across the river stands the large Amphipolis lion.

Some 15 miles beyond the east entrance of the Strimon Gulf is Deftero Cove (Elefthera), a dull but well sheltered large bay with some loading wharves for steamers in the northern corner.

Seven miles E.N.E. is the pleasant modernized commercial port of

Kavalla, (ancient Neapolis), which during modern times has been Greek only for about 50 years, appears from seaward like the Riviera. With a population of nearly fifty thousand, the modern part of the town was built after the First World War to house refugees from Turkey.

Its earlier associations are shewn by the presence of a Roman aqueduct stretching across the town, and the Byzantine fortifications beyond its eastern suburbs. The modern, well-built port is often busy with medium-size steamers in the tobacco transport trade, and during the summer months is active with ferry-boats plying to Thasos with tourists.

Approach and Berth. Chart 1679. There is no difficulty day or night and the most convenient berth is stern to quay near the Post Office.

General. Fresh provisions, fruit and fish are obtainable in abundance. Water by hydrant is cheap; apply at Post Office. Petrol station is nearby. Restaurants are rather primitive and some are attached to the various fish shops along the front.

Officials. As necessary for a Port of Entry.

St Paul landed here on his way to Phillipi, whence a short excursion to the ruins may now be made by car from Kavalla. It was at Phillipi that St Paul gained his first European convert, Lydia, a purple-seller. Also in A.D. 42, two years after the murder of Caesar, Antony and the young Octavian won a decisive victory over Brutus and Cassius.

Thasos is a tall wooded island composed largely of marble, perhaps the most beautiful in the Aegean. Though the green mountains are visible many miles off, the low walls of the old Greek harbour cannot be seen until close to. The navigable channel into Limena (Panayia) harbour is very narrow; but within the port there are depths of 2 fathoms away from the sides. This harbour has recently been officially designated Port Thasos.

Approach and Berth. Chart 1679. This requires great care, for the channel is only 10 yards wide—it is one third of the way between the moleheads from the S.W. Each side of this channel the stone rubble rises sharply, but for 10 yards there is a depth of 15 feet. Both extremities of the moles are lit with fixed green and red lights.

After entering, swing round to N.E. and berth with stern 15 yards from northern mole in about 12 feet.

General. The town of Thasos has several provision shops—10 minutes' walk, and fresh-water taps close to the quays. There are some modern hotels, one or two modest ones and several restaurants. A caique ferry service plies to Kavalla several times a day (one hour), and there are bus services and caique trips around the island.

The beauty of the island is at once apparent—thick forests towering up to the peaks on every side. The ancient Greek town with its amphitheatre,

Macedonian Coast and three northern islands

acropolis and agora, stand out on the hillside immediately above the harbour. It is pleasant to walk up through the olive groves and see this architecture of the past. Modern Thasos with its hotel and restaurants lies on the water-front in the opposite direction.

From the Thasos Strait the low uninteresting coast of Thrace stretches eastwards for 70 miles towards the last Greek port, Alexandroupolis, close to the Turkish frontier.

Alexandroupolis, formerly the wretched shallow Bulgarian port of Dedeagatch, has been improved by the Greeks. It is a shallow lighter port, usually with a swell rolling in from the southward. The small town has become important on account of its communications by air, road, and rail with Turkey. It lies near the mouth of the Evros River, marking the Turkish frontier. This is the largest of the rivers on this coast, and rising in the Bulgarian mountains, flows into the Aegean: these rivers augment the outflow from the Dardanelles and cause a southgoing stream often apparent in certain channels of the Aegean.

On the river estuary are fisheries and on the banks further upstream numerous mulberry groves with a flourishing silk industry.

Alexandroupolis is a Port of Entry. Details are given on Chart 1679.

The islands of Samothrace, Limnos, Strati and Imbros (now Turkish and mentioned later) all belong to the north Aegean.

Raised aloft like a woman's breast.
STRABO

Samothrace (Samothraki) is a single 'lump of marble' rising to over 5,000 feet with steep white cliffs merging into a covering of green woods. Being without a harbour, a precarious landing must be made in the open Kamariotis Bay where the only amenities are a mooring buoy, a rickety pier and a few poor little houses.

The archaeological site at Palaeopolis is in a valley farther round the coast, and can be distinguished from seaward by a Genoese castle on a cliff. It was near this site the Winged Victory, now in the Louvre, was discovered a century ago. Recent interest in excavations by American archaeologists has made it worth while putting up a hostel for visitors.

Samothrace can be reached by a caique-ferry from Alexandroupolis.

Limnos, lying 40 miles to the southward of Thasos, is a dull, sparsely cultivated island, somewhat low-lying with the large harbours of Mudros and Kondia which were used as fleet bases in the First World War, and are of little interest for a yacht today.

Kastro (recently named Merini Kastro) is the only convenient harbour for small vessels and yachts, though this is liable to be crowded with caiques.

Approach and Berth. Chart 1661. There is ample depth when approaching the harbour and quay; a yacht should berth near the extremity of the breakwater, being careful to avoid the half-submerged rocks on which this new quay has been constructed.

Port Facilities are poor. Though fresh provisions can be bought and there is a newly built small hotel, the town is of no interest, and the surrounding country monotonous. Fuel and water are available.

Officials. As necessary for a Port of Entry.

Evstratios or **Strati,** about 17 miles southward of the S.W. corner of Limnos, appears from seaward as a barren hump without interest. It does however grow agricultural produce which is exported only with difficulty, for the island is without a harbour or suitable shelter. Until recently political offenders banished by the Greek Government were sent to this island.

EASTERN SHORES OF THE AEGEAN: *PART I*

ISTANBUL

Sea of Marmara

Gulf of Ismit

Izmit

Marmara Islands

Gulf of Saros

Gelibolu

Lapseki

Artaki (Erdek)

Imroz (Imbros)

Seddulbahr

Chanakkale

Dardanelles

Bozcaada (Tenedos)

Gulf of Endremiti

Ayvalik

Candali

Gulf of Smyrna

IZMIR

Cesme

Sighajik

Kusadasi

Gulf of Mandalya

Budroм

Gulf of Istankoy (or Kos)

Knidas

Gulf of Doris

Marmarice

Gulf of Fetiye

Kas

Fineke

TURKEY

EUROPEAN COAST
and WESTERN SEABOARD of
ANATOLIA

———

PROHIBITED   AREAS

1st. Grade

In the case of the Dardanelles permission for a yacht to anchor off CHANAKKALE and GELIBOLU may be obtained from the commandants of those ports.

2nd. Grade

Permission to anchor off the IZMIR coast may be obtained from the commandant in that city.

Greek territory

It is most important to obtain Clearance when leaving one country and sailing for the other.

4

Eastern Shores of the Aegean

PART I: *DARDANELLES TO SAMOS STRAIT*

GALLIPOLI AND THE DARDANELLES

The western coast of the Gallipoli Peninsula consists of cliffs and sandy beaches with minor indentations suitable for anchoring only in the summer months. The background rises gently to hills of less than a thousand feet largely covered in scrub.

Though Chart 1880 gives plans of both Arapos Bay (Gulf of Saros) and Suvla neither is suitable for yachts—moreover the whole peninsula is a military area and any attempt to anchor here would most certainly be repulsed by armed guards.

It is impossible to sail past these shores without being moved by the sight of the Allied War Cemeteries. More than a dozen burial places of varying sizes were laid out, usually near where men fell in battle—a reminder of our heavy casualties in the campaign of the First World War where a million men fought for possession of the peninsula.

Unlike the usual war cemetery elsewhere, the graves on Gallipoli are marked by plaques of marble lying horizontally on the ground, which is lavishly planted with cypresses and flowering shrubs. The southern end of the peninsula at Cape Helles is marked, not only by a Turkish lighthouse, but by the 70-foot British War Memorial, an obelisk cut in stone shipped from England.

The Passage to Istanbul. From Cape Helles the distance to this former capital of Byzantium is about 150 miles, and much of the route passes through interesting scenery.

The Dardanelles is 25 miles long and from the entrance until well past the Narrows the steep-to European banks are largely covered in scrub with occasional clusters of trees: the land supports only rough grazing. It is sparsely populated except for the small towns mentioned in this chapter.

Although the approach may be made at night this is not recommended; for, added to the embarrassment of steamer traffic, is that of the searchlights at Seddulbahr which like to focus their beams on each approaching vessel. Also, if compelled to anchor off the Cape (a small bay known by the British in the First War as V–Beach) or in Morto Bay, it is certain that the military would

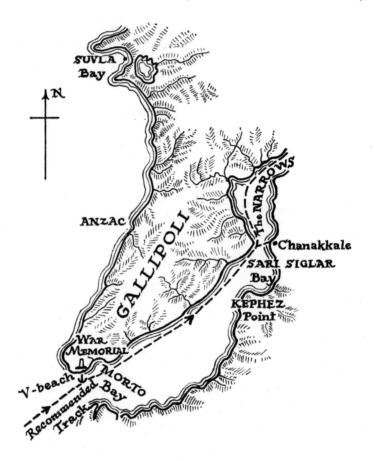

The Dardanelles

interfere—a yacht should therefore aim at entering the Dardanelles soon after dawn to be sure of completing Control formalities and reaching a suitable night anchorage later.

Route. Chart 2429 (with plan) shows that it is practical to follow close under the European shore, thus avoiding the outflowing current. Towards the Narrows this does not exceed 2 knots except in strong north winds when a velocity of 5 knots has been known. All vessels must make for Chanakkale to obtain clearance.

The Current. Sailing vessels seldom used to attempt to sail up the Dardanelles against the current without a fair wind, and often waited outside many days until conditions were favourable. On one occasion in 1807, Duckworth, anxious to press on with his squadron to Constantinople, had to remain at anchor off Tenedos for nine days awaiting a fair wind.

Since the days of Leander many attempts have been made by swimmers to cross from one shore to the other.

On 3 May 1810, Lord Byron in company with a young lieutenant swam from Sestos to the Asiatic shore in one hour ten minutes. On board the frigate *Salsette,* which was at anchor nearby, it was calculated that the distance from the place where they had entered the water on the European shore to the finish of the swim below the Asiatic fort was upwards of 4 miles although the width across the Strait was only one. In the summer of 1923 some naval officers accomplished the swim without difficulty, but in later years the Turks raised official objections to prevent a repetition of the performance.

The chart of the Dardanelles is now marked with the positions of wrecks, some of them British and French battleships sunk by German mines and Turkish guns on 18 March 1915 when the Allies were attempting to fight their way through this vital passage to gain the greater prize of Constantinople. This date was a decisive one for both the Allies and the Turks; for the Allies because they had to abandon any further attempt to force the Dardanelles by warships alone, and were thus compelled to raise a military expeditionary force, while the Turks, profiting by this delay, gained the necessary respite to enable them to continue the war.

On a hillside by the Narrows, in large characters formed of white stones may now been seen '18 March 1915'. But all the forts have vanished, and except for an old Genoese castle there are no visible signs of defensive works today.

Chanakkale, lying on the Asiatic shore of the Narrows, is the Turkish Control Port for all vessels entering or leaving the Dardanelles. Still poor and squalid, it has never been properly repaired since the Allied bombardments of the First War; its ruined houses and dusty streets present a depressing picture to passing ships. Apart from being a Control Port, it is the residence of the Allied Graves Commissioner for the War Cemeteries on Gallipoli.★ He can sometimes arrange for a visit, though only under Turkish supervision.

It is also possible to obtain permission to visit Troy; a car may be hired, and accompanied by a police escort one arrives at the scene of Schliemann's excavations in about an hour.

Anchorage. It is difficult to anchor off the port on account of the steep slope of the seabed and the changing swirls of the current. See chart 2429. Anchor N.N.E. of the loading piers in the deeper water. The two small cambers are suitable only for lighters.

★ Commemorating 40,000 British and Commonwealth dead.

Approaching Nagara above the Narrows, where the width is only a mile, the current usually runs at 2 knots, and rather unexpectedly flows faster at the sides than in the middle. It was here that Xerxes built his bridge of boats for the vast invading army he was leading into Europe in 480 B.C. The bridge crossed a little higher up than Abydos and touched the European shore between Sestos and Madytus. Herodotus wrote: 'And now as he looked and saw the whole Hellespont covered with the vessels of his fleet and all the shore and every plain about Abydos as full as possible of men, Xerxes congratulated himself upon his good fortune; but after a little while he wept.' It was at Abydos where Alexander first set foot in Asia.

Today there is almost nothing to be seen at Sestos and only a few poor dwellings at Abydos, one of which, now a petrol dump, was the house where Byron stayed on his voyage from Smyrna to Constantinople:

> *The winds are high on Helle's wave*
> *As on the night of stormy water*
> *When love, who sent, forgot to save*
> *The young—the beautiful—the brave.*
> *The lonely hope of Sestos' daughter.*

In the Dardanelles twenty foreign steamers may be passed in the day,[*] proceeding to or from Istanbul or the Black Sea ports, of which almost half may be flying the flag of Iron Curtain countries. Local caiques are also to be seen, ferrying either passengers or cattle from one shore to the other. Also some Turkish steamers mostly in the coastal trade. Farther northwards the undulating countryside on the banks becomes more attractive, and in early summer yellow-brown cornfields suggest England at its best.

Continuing up the Dardanelles it will be necessary for a sailing yacht to find an anchorage for the night, as the breeze drops immediately after sunset. Two suitable places, both out of the current are:

Lapseki, on the Asiatic shore, is a country town with a roadstead protected by a stone pier. There is convenient anchorage off the pier's extremity in 3 fathoms, well sheltered except between N.W. and N.E. In event of winds from this quarter proceed to Gallipoli shore and anchor under the old town on the hill now named Gelibolu.

Lapseki, now a small modern town, was once the sacred city of the Priapus cult.

---

[*] In the Straits of Dover more than 700 vessels, including British, pass in a day.

Gelibolu Bay. Anchor in N.W. corner near a stone pier by a clump of trees in 3 fathoms. There is a hospital with an officers' mess nearby.

Though both these places are in the prohibited area, the Turkish Commandant usually allows a yacht to stay here for the night.

Sea of Marmara. Yachts proceeding into this sea will find some suitable anchorages for the night at the Marmara Islands and at Artaki, a recently developed resort. But when making the passage to Istanbul it is advisable to sail close under the northern shore, in order to take advantage of the better breezes and smooth water. By night there is normally a moderate land breeze.

Princes Islands. There are six, of which only two are of interest and were better known by their former Greek names:

(a) **Antigone** (now **Burgaz**) is a summer bathing place reached by ferry in an hour from Istanbul. It has an anchorage off the ferry pier, though there is better shelter behind a sunken mole whose root lies 100 yards south of this pier.

(b) **Prinkipo** (now **Buyukada**) is the largest and most fashionable of these islands with many summer villas. The anchorage off the town is rather exposed, but better shelter can be obtained in Yurukali Bay behind the promontory projecting from the western shore.

The other four islands are of no interest to a yacht; Plati (Yassiada) being a naval base should not be approached too closely.

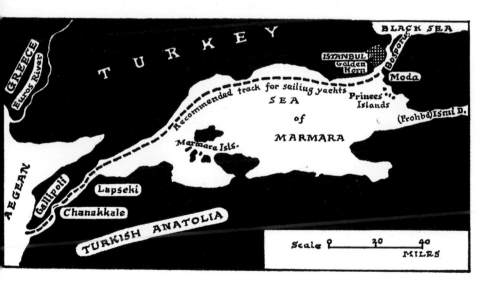

Istanbul. Chart 2286. Yachts on arrival should anchor off Dolma Badche out of the tideway and haul their sterns into the quay. While port formalities are being completed, one may watch the never-ending flow of traffic: large steamers, local craft, and fast motor-boats all straining to enter or leave the Bosporus and Golden Horn. After obtaining clearance it is convenient to anchor in comparative peace in the open bay of **Moda** near the Yacht Club Deniz. In summer, apart from wash caused by the ferry-boats, the sea here is undisturbed.

Facilities. Club Deniz can be most helpful to a foreign yacht. All provisions, ice etc. can be obtained.

Water is available from a tap in the boat harbour, and it is possible for a yacht to berth near the head of a small pier and take in water by hose.

A small repair shop is available at the Club, both for limited shipwright work and sail-making.

Petrol and diesel fuel can be obtained in drums or one's own cans.

A good ferry service calls close by and reaches Galata Bridge in 20 minutes.

> *Tall minarets, shining mosques, barbaric towers,*
> *Fountains and palaces, and cypress bowers.*
> HEMANS

The City. Guide-books explain the many interesting places to be seen in Istanbul, yet one is apt to forget that this city with its 1¼ million population has only recently acquired a western look. As late as the twenties the alleys and bazaars were crowded with men nearly all wearing the red fez and clad in Asian costume. There were Arabs, Persians, Kurds, Armenians, Circassians and Greeks, all to be distinguished by their dress. The few women to be seen were veiled. In the narrow streets were Dervishes, lemonade-sellers with their huge brass apparatus, story-tellers, letter-writers and barrel-organ players. Threading their way through this gossiping crowd, would pass the laden donkeys with their drivers, and porters bearing heavy loads.

On 1 November 1922, these outward signs of an eastern world began to change, for Kemal Attaturk had come to power. By deposing the Sultan many centuries of ancient Turkish tradition and customs were discarded. A new democratic state arose with the Gregorian calendar, metric system, handwriting in Latin characters and western clothes. Almost over-night the fez and the veil were swept away and the power of holy men and priests abolished.

The Bosporus, 16 miles in length and in places only 1,700 yards wide, is remarkable not only for its beauty but for its many types of ships and local craft. On account of the 3-knot current and the unpredictable whirlpools, it is advisable to proceed under power. Though permission to enter the Bosporus is not required, no vessels may proceed into the Black Sea without notifying the Turkish authorities, and at the same time a study should be made of the position of the net obstruction and the prohibited areas.

Fishing. (See also under *General Information*.) Few people realize the quantity of fish to be found in these waters and in the Marmara. Over 80 varieties are said to exist and yet fishing has been as little exploited here as at other places on the Anatolian coast. The mackerel, according to local opinion, are unsurpassed in quality anywhere, and this is believed to be due largely to an abundance of plankton on which the sardine and anchovy feed; they are eaten by the mackerel which in turn is devoured by the bonito. Tunny frequent these waters and occasionally the blue shark.

The tunny which pass into the Mediterranean early in spring are keenly fished off Sardinia, Sicily and other places before they reach the Aegean and Black Sea to spawn. They enter the Black Sea along the coast of Asia and return along that of Europe, a peculiarity noted by Pliny who, following a theory of Aristotle, supposed that the fish see better through the right eye than the left!

The Anatolian Coast. Leaving Istanbul to visit this coast one is apt to expect the veneer of western culture, so apparent in the capital, to be encountered elsewhere. It will soon be found that it is not. Among the more primitive surroundings western influence has made no headway against the traditional Turkish outlook; although friendly and courteous to the westerner it is soon apparent that Turkish officials have a fundamental oriental suspicion of any foreigner.

FROM THE DARDANELLES—SOUTHWARD

THE ISLANDS

Emerging from the mouth of the Dardanelles and turning to the southward a vessel passes the green valley of Troy and Beshika Bay, and the anchorage where sailing vessels bound for Constantinople sometimes had to await a fair wind.

The small, flat and uninteresting island of Tenedos lies close off the Anatolian coast and, together with Imbros in the north, forms the sentinels guarding the Hellespont approach. Both were advance bases of the Allies in the First World War and are the only Aegean islands held by the Turks. Whereas Imbros is partly wooded and hilly, with two alternative partially sheltered anchorages, Tenedos is flat and rather bare with a small 2-fathom port, formerly defended by a well-preserved Genoese castle.

Tenedos (Bozcaada in Turkish). In Byzantine days when Constantinople was dependent upon its corn supplies from Egypt, ships frequently had long delays off Tenedos awaiting a favourable wind to blow them up the Dardanelles. To avoid this idleness of valuable shipping Justinian had a huge granary built to enable vessels to unload there and then return to Egypt for another cargo. Small

71

freighters then ferried the grain up to Constantinople as opportunity offered. Nothing is left of the granary today; and the vineyards, which 200 years ago were so famous, have largely vanished and produce but little wine for export. The island, now poor, still has its derelict little harbour to provide shelter for trading caiques.

Approach and Berth. Chart 1608. The two breakwaters have been largely destroyed by gales, but their extremities are clearly to be discerned a mile off. The red oil-lamp at the head of the southern mole shows barely half a mile. It is advisable to anchor in the centre of the harbour in $2\frac{1}{2}$ fathoms and then take a long warp ashore. Though open to east, the harbour is quite comfortable in normal weather.

Officials—the island has a Governor, Customs and Police who do not appreciate a visit by a foreign yacht.

Suggested cruise down Anatolia coast

Lesbos: Port Sigri

Amphorae from Sifnos being landed at Port Sigri

TWO AEGEAN SANDY
BEACHES

Koukunarias on Skiathos

Tsamadou beach on Samos

Facilities. Spring water suitable for drinking is available, but must be carried some distance. There are a couple of poor quality provision shops where food is sometimes rationed.

Leaving Tenedos and pointing southwards down the straight Anatolian coast a sailing yacht, helped by the south-going current and a fresh north wind in the summer months, is quickly blown towards the impressive steep-to Cape Baba. Here a decision must be made whether to follow the Turkish coast towards the

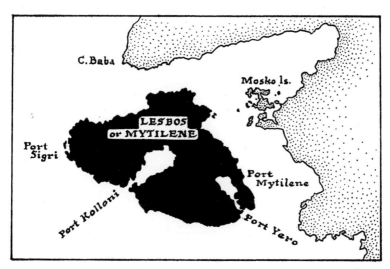

Edremiti Gulf (with Aivalik and the Mosko Islands) or turn towards the island of Mytilene (Lesbos).

During the Meltemi season the wind now turns to the west, and again follows the Turkish coast into the gulf usually maintaining its strength until sunset.

About 5 miles past the Cape is the ancient port of Assos (now called Behram by the Turks) with its two moles still showing above water. It is now too shallow for a yacht of medium draft, but a few local boats use it. St Paul embarked here after visiting Troy and was rowed southwards on his third missionary journey in A.D. 71.

> *'This noble and pleasant Island'.*
> STRABO

Mytilene (Mitilene, Lesbos) is large and mountainous; now officially known as Lesbos. The eastern part of the island is green and wooded, but the land around the coast on the western side is poor and partially arid. The island attracts many Greek visitors in the summer months.

There are four harbours:

(*a*) **Port Mytilene,** the capital, is a pleasant little town in a delightful setting of partially green mountains, with a port for caiques, fishing craft and local steamers from Piraeus.

> **Approach and Berth.** Chart 1664. Enter the Southern Harbour and berth stern to the broad quay near the Port Office. Yachts sometimes berth outside the port near the root of the mole, where in summer it is cooler.
>
> **General.** There is a good fresh-water hydrant and a hose supplied by the harbour office. There are plenty of good shops for fresh provisions, and a palatable dry wine may be bought locally. There are some restaurants on the water-front and two modest hotels. Clean hot baths and showers are to be had in a street leading off from the Park. There are plenty of taxis. Mechanical repairs can be undertaken by Firestone which is also a petrol depot.
>
> A Port of Entry; there are Health, Immigration, Customs and Harbour officials.
>
> A daily steamer runs from Piraeus, and then sails for Chios; there is also an air service to Athens five times a week in summer. A caique runs once a week to the Turkish port of Aivalik.
>
> In the town, apart from the Genoese castle and Museum there is not much to see; but to offset this, a number of delightful drives may be taken to the country, passing through mountain forests and many olive groves from which the island derives much of its limited prosperity.

In antiquity the island was made famous by Aesop who wrote many of his stories here, and by Sappho, who is believed to have been born at Eresos, a village on the S.W. coast; it was here she wrote her poems.

(*b*) **Port Sigri** on the west coast is a convenient place to shelter from the Meltemi, but not worth a special visit.

> **Approach and Berth.** Chart 1671 is best, though 1664 is adequate together with *Sailing Directions* in giving a view of the approach.
>
> There is good protection from the N.E. wind and sea in the bay southward of Sigri village, when the old castle bears N.W. and the depth is 3 to 4 fathoms. The caiques also berth here, and in the event of northerly winds run a warp ahead to the rocks on shore, for the holding (thin weed or very hard sand) is poor. It appears that there is a hard layer of rock immediately under the sand, into which anchor flukes will not bite. There is better holding in the more remote N.E. corner of the bay, and often the caiques shelter here in N.E. gales.
>
> **General.** The village of 600 people is very poor. They were originally brought over from the Asian coast in exchange for the former Turkish inhabitants after the First War.
>
> There is bus communication with Mytilene town every other day—3 hours.
>
> Bread, eggs and vegetables are obtainable, otherwise supplies must be ordered from Mytilene—a 2-day delay.
>
> Water is piped to the village from a spring, and is good, but the few taps are rather far from the landing place.
>
> A rough track ascends to Mount Ordymnos which can be reached in 3 hours. From the monastery on the summit there is a grand view of the distant islands.

(*c*) **Port Kolloni** on the south coast has an interesting mountainous entrance leading into a dull expanse of sheltered water.

Approach. Chart 1668. This is narrow, yet easy by day, for both good leading marks and buoys are now established. Certain lights are exhibited at night, but they should not be relied upon.

Anchorage. Apoteka Bay is well sheltered from the Meltemi. The holding is good (mud) and the sea is cooled by fresh water from the river.

General. There are a few small cottages near the cove, but they are partly deserted. Some fishermen are based here in summer.

(*d*) **Port Yero** is more suitable as a Fleet anchorage than for yachts. The approach and narrow entrance are attractive, and there are one or two coves here which afford convenient anchorage.

> *Leave battles to the Turkish hordes and shed the blood of Scio's★ Vine.*
>
> BYRON

Chios with its population of 26,000 is slowly declining. Cultivation has also deteriorated and the island is barely self-supporting, though formerly it had a large export of mastic, herbs and oranges as well as considerable shipping. A guide-book written early in the last century described it as 'the most beautiful most fertile, richest and most severely afflicted of the Aegean islands'.

★ Scio was the name given to the island by the Venetians, and its wine has been considered of high quality since antiquity.

Approaching the eastern coast the island stands out mountainous and bare, and on landing it appears today less beautiful, less fertile and certainly not as rich as some of the others.

There are one or two excursions within easy reach by car. Perhaps the most profitable is to drive over the hills to the remarkable Byzantine monastery at Neo Moni with its notable mosaics. The 'School of Homer' with its rotund topped rock, and the poet's alleged birthplace, 3 miles north of the town, are of moderate interest.

The drive to Pyrghi with its medieval walls, and the mastic groves close by, is also rewarding.

(a) **Port Chios**

Approach and Berth. Chart 1568. The entrance is easy by day or night. The harbour is large and well sheltered with broad quays and a busy little town close beside them. The most convenient berth is stern to the quay immediately to the westward of the entrance. Steamers berth near the Customs House.

Officials. A Port of Entry. Customs, Health, Immigration and Police, whose offices are on the quay.

Port Facilities. Fresh water was reported not to be as good as at most islands. Provision shops are close by. Two modest hotels are close to the quay, also a restaurant; and Bona Vista, a summer resort southwards along the front provides a dining place with a cabaret. A new first class hotel was opened in 1960.

The Piraeus steamer calls daily on its circuit to Mytilene and Kavalla and a caique runs once a week to Cesme on the Turkish coast.

Historical. During the past centuries the people of Chios have roused the admiration of a number of travellers largely on account of their marked ascendency over the inhabitants of other Aegean islands. In the seventeenth century travellers remarked that after Constantinople and Smyrna, Chios was the most wealthy and civilized place in the Turkish Empire. Their women had the reputation of being exceptionally good-looking, and Lithgo, a Scot, writing at this period, records:

> The Women of the Citty of Sio [its former spelling] are the most beautiful Dames or rather Angelicall creatures of all Greeks, upon the face of the earth, and greatly given to Venery. Their Husbands are their Pandors, and when they see any stranger arrive, they will presently demand of him; if he would have a Mistresse: and so they make Whoores of their own wives ... If a stranger be desirous to stay all night with any of them, their price is a chicken of Gold, nine shillings English, out of which their companion receiveth his supper, and for his pains a belly full of sinful content.

At the beginning of the nineteenth century when the island was thriving on its valuable exports, many wealthy Greek families enjoyed the general high standard then prevailing. In the ill-fated year of 1822 the inhabitants were encouraged to revolt against their Turkish masters who, retaliating quickly, ruthlessly killed twenty-five thousand people and carried off forty-five thousand inhabitants. The French artist Delacroix painted an imaginative picture of this gruesome event: it is now in the Louvre. Though this calamity wrecked the social structure of the island, vengeance soon came and the spirit of revolt revived when the

Greek Admiral Canaris led a small naval squadron with two fireships into the harbour by night and destroyed two large Turkish warships, one with two thousand men on board. General Gordon describes this feat as 'one of the most extraordinary military exploits in history'. The statue to Constantine Canaris is in the park, and there are ships named after this modern Greek hero today. The most recent 'affliction' was a terrible earthquake in the eighties when five thousand inhabitants were killed.

The Growing of Mastic. For more than two thousand years there was great trade with the east in mastic. This is obtained by making incisions in the branches of these six-foot shrubs and draining the sticky fluid into little cups—according to Pliny it is like 'Frankinscense adulterated with resin'. That most highly praised was the white mastic of Chios which in later years had the entire monopoly for supplying the Turkish Empire and consequently brought much wealth to the Chians. The death-knell came when Turkish ladies ceased to chew mastic and other substances took its place in the paint market. Now the culture of these shrubs has declined and this, together with the recession in other industries has brought poverty to the island and induced considerable emigration to countries in the west.

(*b*) **Evorias,** on the south side of the island, is a charming small cove lying between two hills and sheltered on three sides. A few cottages and a taverna have recently sprung up by the shore. Some vineyards and groves of mastic shrubs add to the attraction of this peaceful scene.

Approach and Anchorage. This small cove—400 yards in depth—is unmarked on the chart, but is easy to find. It lies close westward of Cape Kamari, which may be recognized, not by a 'monastery ruin' (shown on chart) but by a couple of modern stone huts. There are no lights. The bottom is of clear sand and runs out 300 yards to depths of 3 or 4 fathoms. There is 2 fathoms depth about 100 yards off a small stone pier in the centre of the bay with barely room to swing—a warp ashore is recommended. The day breeze blows off the land. The cove is sheltered on three sides and open only to S.E.

General. A British archaeological expedition dug some trenches here in 1955 and recovered certain Hellenic pottery now to be seen in the Chios museum. Skin-divers also made an exploration of the seabed.

Fishermen use the cove as a base during the summer months.

(*c*) **Kolokithia Bay** is also a sheltered anchorage, used by caiques, but has nothing to commend it for a yacht.

(*d*) **Oinousai Islands** or **Spalmatori.** These barren, hilly islands projecting from the east coast of Chios have some small bays on the southern shores where a yacht may lie for the night or ride in comfort during the Meltemi:

Pasha Bay. Chart 1568. Here is a sandy bottom with good holding in 6 fathoms.

The only sign of habitation is a farmhouse, and some cultivation in the valleys where vines and figs are grown. In the spring there is sufficient grass on the slopes for goats to graze.

Mandraki, the only village in the group, has a thousand inhabitants, many of whom live here only part of the year. Two modern buildings, a naval school and a technical school may be seen close to the shore.

Anchorage. On the northern side of the cove is a landing pier with provision shops nearby. The anchorage off the pier is sheltered from prevailing winds, but the holding being soft sand with boulders, is rather uncertain.

The only officials here are Police.

Psara, lying 10 miles west of Chios, is a small primitive island seldom visited by a yacht.

There is a good shelter on the south side of the principal village in 2-fathom depths protected by a recently extended mole. (Chart 1568)

Communication with Volissos, the N.W. side of Chios is maintained by caique.

The few inhabitants of this barren little island are still traditionally seamen. Psara's claim to fame is on account of its being the birthplace of Admiral Canaris, Greece's naval hero in the War of Independence.

> *Thus all their forces being joined together, they hoisted saile towards the Isle of Samos and there gave themselves to feasts and solace.*
> PLUTARCH, writing of Antony and Cleopatra

Samos The large wooded and mountainous island of Samos, separated by barely a mile from the Turkish mainland is one of the most attractive in the Aegean. Since the days of Polycrates it has been famous for its forests and vine-

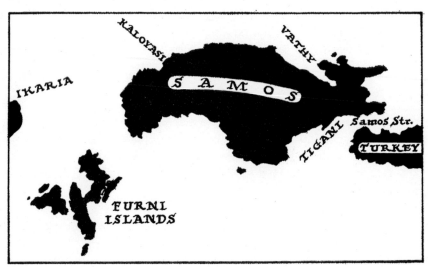

yards. It still provides the timber for most of the caiques built in the Aegean, and offers both a good dry wine and an indifferent type of Malmvoisie imported into England today. The pottery for which in Hellenic days Samos was world-famous must not be confused with the dull-red 'Samian Ware' sometimes dug up by archaeologists on Roman sites in England. This pottery, though it took the name from Samos, was imported into England by Roman merchants in the first century A.D. and was actually made in France.

Today there are 60,000 inhabitants in Samos distributed among a number of hill villages as well as the three major ports.

(a) Kalovasi at the N.W. end of the island is an uninteresting artificial port which, in a northerly gale, is untenable; but it has some lovely country behind with attractive mountain villages.

Approach. Chart 1568. There is no difficulty day or night. Harbour lights are established on either mole-head.

Berth with stern to the quay 50 yards east of steamer quay, bows north; here is about 2 fathoms near the quay, some of which has crumbled away.

General. There are very few provision shops. Water, which is good, can be bought from a lorry or obtained in cans.

A daily steamer calls from Piraeus, and cargo vessels collect shipments of timber and wine.

The effect of northerly gales has caused much silting of the beach lying to the eastward of the southern mole.

(b) Port Vathy is a secure anchorage off the capital of Samos; it is protected by a short mole, but rather exposed to swell from winds in the northerly quadrant. The harbour is now known officially as Port Samos.

Approach and Anchorage. Chart 1530. There is no difficulty day or night.

Let go in 3 or 4 fathoms anywhere convenient behind the breakwater. There are rings on the quayside where the steamers used to secure their sterns and sometimes caiques do so today; but there is no advantage in securing a yacht in this way here. Holding is good, but in strong N.W. winds a swell comes in. Land in the dingy anywhere off this long quay which has now become an esplanade. Steamers berth alongside at the quay on the mole where a berth has been dredged, but elsewhere the quaysides have silted.

General. Customs and harbour offices are close to the root of the mole, and in 1960 there was still a British Vice-Consul here, this being the only British consular post remaining in the Aegean Islands.

Water from the quay on the mole can be obtained with difficulty, for running water is scarce and in summer is turned on only for 1 hour. There are plenty of shops for fresh provisions, a new first class hotel (1960) and several restaurants and cafés. There is steamer communication with Piraeus via Ikaria and Mykonos; bus services to other places on the island along a good coastal road, and across to Tigani.

Despite the wine presses and tobacco factories trade here, and elsewhere in Samos, is declining.

(c) **Tigani** (Pythagorion). A shallow, but well-sheltered little port of great antiquity beside a pleasant small village.

Approach and Berth. Chart 1530 shows the essential features. By night it is advisable to anchor in the outer harbour. Chart 1878 is from an old survey and is inaccurate for depths. Shoal water extends from S.W. corner of the inner harbour and a square beacon on a platform (unlit) marks the N.E. corner of this shoal.

Pass through the middle of the channel between above mentioned beacon and southern extremity of mole in 12 feet depth. Proceed to northward of some steps in the quay (where

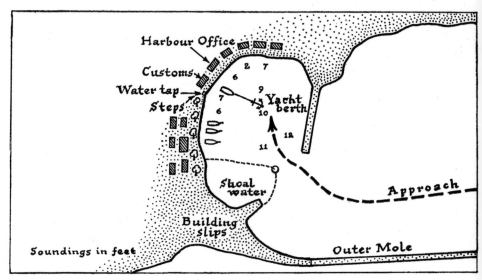

Port Tigani. During Meltemi strong gusts come off the mountains above but the harbour is immune

there is a depth of 8 feet) and lay out anchor to E.S.E. in 10 feet. There are plenty of iron rings nearby. During the Meltemi, though gusts come down the mountains nearby with gale strength, the wind is moderate in the harbour.

Officials. This is a Port of Entry with the usual authorities.

General. There is a fresh water tap under an Ionic marble capital nearby. Though a poor little village, there is a small inn with running water, a restaurant and one or two bar/cafés. The quay is well shaded with eucalyptus trees and mulberries. Ice is available and petrol can be bought. The place is very clean. A bus runs to Port Vathy (Samos) and taxis are available.

The little port is now decaying from its former status, but it is a centre for excursions to several ancient monuments and sites.

Recently the Greek Government decided to rename Tigani (which it had been called for centuries) Pythagorion in honour of the great mathematician's birthplace.

There is rich farming country in the broad valley to the westward, vines, tobacco and corn being grown extensively.

Early History. At Tigani, Herodotus was impressed by the three 'great works' of Polycrates, which are still to be seen today. In the port itself, the inner harbour is much as Polycrates built it, and on the hill above can be seen the Hellenic walls, 14 feet thick, which encompassed the old city of Heraion. A large number of drums of columns and some capitals from the buildings of the old city have been plundered from the ruins and brought to the port for use as bollards, stands for water-taps and sometimes flower-pot stands outside the houses. The famous water-tunnel, now 2,500 years old, is interesting though difficult to explore and one cannot emerge at the other end, as it is blocked; its irregularity and the slippery nature of the limestone ledges have sometimes brought the most intrepid visitors to disaster. It is necessary to provide oneself with taper flares and a torch, and to obtain the services of a guide from the village.

An interesting motor drive leads to the ruins of the temple of Hera along the coast. New roads in the island have been under construction recently and in 1960 one was advancing towards the mouth of the tunnel; this doubtless heralds the approach of many charabancs in the years to come.

Tigani has been tidied up in recent years. It has much charm, and in the coolness of a summer evening it is pleasant to be on the water-front enjoying an evening meal under the eucalyptus trees.

(*d*) **Marathokambos** is yet a fourth harbour lying on the south-west coast, but it is very little used partly on account of storm damage, and because of the violent squalls off the high mountains during the summer months.

Ikaria (sometimes spelt Nicaria) is a large tall, island only 5 miles west of Samos. Though it has a pleasant village, the island is seldom visited by yachts as it has no harbour. There are a couple of sandy coves on the southern shores used by the mail-steamer from Piraeus—these open anchorages are susceptible to strong squalls during the Meltemi.

THE TURKISH COAST

The coast from the Dardanelles, extending southwards past Troy and Tenedos, and then eastwards beyond Cape Baba as far as Assos, has been described in the last chapter.

This coast now continues eastward, broken by the Edremiti gulf and the arid Mosko Islands. Here in Roman days (when they were known as Poroselene) Pausanias was an eye-witness of the spectacle of a tame dolphin that came at a boy's call and allowed him to ride on its back. Though confirmed by another witness this story still raises doubt as to its credibility, even though the dolphin was always regarded by the early Greeks as a friend and was not hunted.

An 11-foot channel—Taliani on the British chart—now leads to the port of

Aivali. Known now as Aivalik (Turkish) it is a poor little town of 3,000 people who thrive on the export of its high-grade olive oil and soap.

Aivalik

Approach. Chart 1672. The interesting narrow Taliani channel is irregular in width and depth, but some attempt to maintain this channel is indicated by the placing of new beacons in 1955 and a flashing light on Rowley Point.

Anchorage. A newly arrived yacht must anchor off the Customs House (just north of the protruding land with a club and cinema) in a depth of about 5 fathoms. The bottom is mud and is good holding.

Officials. Being a Port of Entry, there are Health, Police, Immigration and Customs, with the usual Turkish bureaucratic formalities.

Port Facilities. There is no convenient place to land in a dinghy. The resulting sea from the day breeze, which during summer blows force 5 from the west from noon until two hours after sunset, makes boat work almost impossible; only in the forenoon is it calm during Meltemi conditions.

There is no good water available, though piped water from a distant spring is likely to be

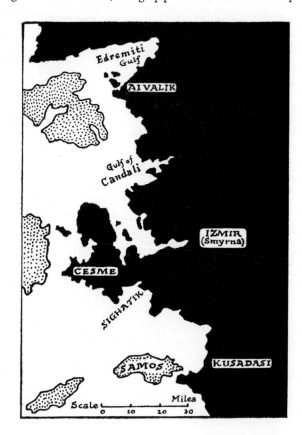

laid on shortly. Fresh fruit, bread and meat may be bought in the market and shops. There is a bank, an hotel (without piped water), a cinema, a restaurant and a club. Ice and petrol can be bought.

A steamer from Izmir calls weekly and buses to Izmir run three times a day (3½ hours).

There is a fine bathing beach the S.W. side of the bay. On the surrounding hills and islands can be seen the ruins of some old monasteries.

A car may be hired for the drive to the ancient city of Pergamon. The road is fast, and the hour's drive well merits this interesting visit. Its original port was at Dikeli at the head of the gulf of Candali, opposite the south coast of Mitilene. From here the river Caicus formerly provided an artery of transport to the ancient city—a distance of about 15 miles. There have been conflicting reports on the suitability of the present anchorage for leaving a yacht when visiting the ancient city, and probably Aivalik is the safer place.

Since Pergamon's period of greatness (second century B.C.) the river has dried up and there is now a road along its old course by which one can drive to the city. As one approaches it can be noted that nothing above ground level remains, but its foundations reveal something of the vastness of this 'Athens of Asia'.

The modern Bergama, a substantial town, is built on the site of the former residential part of the great Greek and Roman cities. It lies at the foot of the Acropolis, on whose steep slopes stand the crumbling tiers of seats of the Greek theatre and the foundations of Greek, Roman and Byzantine walls. Seen from the top, in the light of the setting sun, the view across the ruins to the green fertile plain is magnificent.

The famous Great Altar of Zeus, discovered in the seventies of the last century south of the Acropolis, was excavated mostly by Dörpfeld and removed to the Kaiser Frederick Museum, Berlin, Carried off by the Russians after the Second World War this massive altar with its fine friezes was returned in 1957 and has been re-erected in the Pergamon Museum, East Berlin.

As well as the massive basilica of Hadrian's time there are across the river-bed remains of a Roman theatre and the more remarkable Aesculapium of the 4th century B.C.

Historical. Our word 'parchment' is derived from the name Pergamon. According to Pliny, the Ptolemies of Egypt, becoming jealous of the growing importance of the Pergamon library, prohibited the export of papyrus from Egypt. This compelled the king of Pergamon to revert to the former use of animal skins for writing upon; but he demanded improvements in the technique, as a result the more delicate skins of calf and kid came to be used and adapted for writing on both sides. This eventually became known as vellum.

Izmir or **Smyrna.** To enter this gulf involves a lengthy detour from the Aegean and with the strong prevailing N.W. wind in summer it may take a long time to work back. Although the shores of the gulf are comparatively interesting, Izmir, Turkey's second largest port, is an uninspiring city, and an uncomfortable place for a yacht to berth.

Approach and Berth. Chart 1522. There is no difficulty day or night, the only sheltered berth is in the old port.

Berth near the harbour office, bows west and stern to the quay among the local boats and caiques. The 'Imbat' (similar to the Meltemi) blows force 6 every afternoon from the west; it is advisable to lay out an anchor with plenty of cable. Bottom is hard mud. Large ferry steamers are constantly passing, and berth close by.

Port Officials A Port of Entry. Health, Harbour, Police, Customs and Immigration, all of whom are over-burdened with red tape.

Port Facilities. Provisions, petrol and tap water (not tested) are close at hand. A pleasant dry Smyrna wine may be bought locally. Taxis are available close by. The British Consulate-General is about 1 mile northward on the seafront, and an adequate modern hotel is passed on the way.

The town, though largely rebuilt after the great Fire, is of no particular interest. The drive to the magnificent ruins of Ephesus★ (1¼ hours), passing through pleasant country, is a rewarding excursion.

The new harbour at Daragac Burnu (1¼ miles northward) was completed in 1961 and all steamers now berth here. The few local yachts moor northward of this port close under the shore. There is a ferry service.

Historical. For three centuries Smyrna was a centre for British and French Levant trade, and for many years a naval guardship was stationed here, and a shore hospital maintained. The large Greek colony was a flourishing community.

After the defeat of Turkey in the First World War Smyrna suddenly became a focal point of world interest when the Greeks, seizing this opportunity, landed a military force to invade Turkey. Unexpectedly rallied by Kemal, the Turkish army routed the Greeks, who, retreating in disorder, fled towards Smyrna. Here a massacre of Christians was followed by a complete evacuation of Greeks—largely by allied warships. Nearly a million people were carried by sea from Smyrna to be settled at a number of places on the Greek mainland.

The comparatively settled conditions today support a belief that the rich hinterland with its increasing agricultural produce and improved technique in mining valuable ores will ensure the port's prosperity. To maintain its safe navigational access, the river, which at one time was threatening to block the channel, has now been diverted away from the town.

Iskalesi. A small fishing harbour on the corner of the Gulf, also used by a few sailing people of Izmir.

Approach and Berth. Chart 1617. The harbour, which is very small, is easy to find by day, for there is a large stumpy white tower on its extremity. No harbour lights.

With nearly 3 fathoms in the entrance there is sufficient depth to berth stern to the outer extremity of the mole where shelter is all-round. It is however more convenient to anchor in the wide bay on the eastern side of the island, off the hospital. Here there is good holding on sand, and shelter from the summer 'Imbat'.

★ See under Kusadasi, page 86.

General. The village seems a poor little place and supports only a few fishermen. A bus runs to Izmir and ferry-steamers sometimes call.

The island of Kiladozmen, once the quarantine island for Izmir, affords a couple of suitable anchorages according to the wind; the harbour of Urla is not worth entering when satisfactory shelter can be got outside. The island has a series of hospital buildings for patients with diseases of the bone.

Though some of the Urla Islands are in the military zone, Kiladozmen is not; but it is advisable to inform the authorities at Izmir of an intended visit.

Çesme is a bay, open to the west, with a poor village overlooked by a Genoese castle.

Approach. Chart 1617. The Kaloyer reef which is easy to avoid is now marked on its S.E. corner by a short post.

Anchorage. Let go about 1 cable west of the Customs House with the Dervish tomb bearing about N.W. The coast to the northward deflects the sea caused by the local N.W. sea-breeze, and the wind does not blow home. The bottom here is mud and sand.

Officials. Health, Customs, Immigration and Police.

Port Facilities. There is no convenient landing place, though it is normally possible to land and leave the dinghy at the quay with the Police. There are a few shops for vegetables, and ice can be obtained.

From the village, a fast road leads to Ilicak and thence to Izmir. A passenger caique connects with Chios 3 or 4 times weekly.

Historical. Though the castle is deserted today, its defenders 200 years ago witnessed a heart-rending battle when almost the whole Turkish fleet was annihilated by three powerful Russian squadrons. Having refitted in England, they had sailed out from the Baltic to operate independently in the Mediterranean. After seeking the Turks elsewhere in Aegean waters the Russians found them on 5 July 1770, at anchor off Çesme, and immediately brought them to action.

The Russian victory was complete, and not without interest to the British. On board the Russian ships were Admirals Elphinstone and Greig, while of the three fire-ships which caused such havoc, two of them had British captains.

Sighajik (ancient Teos). From Çesme it is 38 miles down the coast to the ruins of the Ionian city of Teos. Proceeding southwards and rounding Cape Bianco, the course takes one to the S.E. and into the Gulf of Sighajik, at the head of which is a sheltered anchorage. The ruins of the ancient quays and much scattered masonry are still to be seen with the help of Chart 1606.

Kusadasi is the nearest anchorage for Ephesus. It consists of a partially sheltered roadstead with a small town, and a road to the ancient city.

Approach. Chart 1546 with plan, is largely out of date except for the depths. The Petrona reef and Karakaci bank should be given a wide berth.

Anchorage. Vessels anchor between the island of Kus and the buildings ashore. There is about $3\frac{1}{2}$ fathoms 200 yards from the shore when the minaret bears 140°. Bottom is sand and the holding good. Shelter here is better than one might expect with the usual westerly day breeze up to a strength of force 6 during the afternoon. The wind does not blow home, and the sea is largely broken by the outlying reefs and the island. By night the wind blows gently from the east, though there are also occasions when it comes from the north, which then makes the anchorage very uncomfortable.

Should the anchorage become untenable it may be advisable to make for **Murtia Bay,** Samos.

Officials. Harbour-master, Customs and Police.

Port Facilities. In 1960 it was reported that a substantial pier had been built projecting seaward from the former landing place.

Though there is piped water in the town, people buy drinking water in carafes; it is carried in from a special spring.

Recently a summer hotel has been built to encourage tourists, who bathe along the lengthy sandy beach. There is a large café on the front and other bars and small hotels along the beach beyond the town. At the few shops, bread, meat, vegetables and fruit may be bought. Ice and petrol are available.

The main Izmir—Aydin highway passes through, and there is a bus service to Ephesus.

In 1955 the town had a population of 6,000 mostly engaged in olive oil industry and agriculture.

A car may be hired to drive to Ephesus, a journey of 30 minutes. The ruins are interesting and extensive; at least half a day should be allowed to see what is left of this once greatest city in Asia with its temple, a former Wonder of the World.

Ephesus. The road follows the old course of the Cayster River, along which St Paul was rowed when visiting Ephesus nineteen centuries ago. Now completely silted, part of it has become meadows where the camels graze. Outside Ephesus the old harbour has become a marsh but the quays can still be traced. From here a broad street, perfectly preserved and paved with marble, leads up to the city and the large amphitheatre, estimated to hold an audience of 25,000.

Historical. It is easy to re-create here the historic occasion of the demonstration by the silversmiths after St Paul had been preaching here for some months. Summoned by their leader, Demetrius, they met together to protest against the ruin of their souvenir trade in selling small silver goddesses to the Roman tourists. They became infuriated against St Paul and a riot ensued. Rushing into the amphitheatre they shouted 'Great is Diana of the Ephesians'.*

Even in Greek and Roman days this 'largest emporium of Asia Minor' had its difficulties in keeping the river navigable for sea-borne trade. Strabo writes:

'The mouth of the harbour was made narrower by the engineers, but they, along with the king who ordered it, were deceived as to the result—for he thought the entrance would be deep enough for large vessels . . . if a mole were thrown up at the mouth which was very

---

* Acts of the Apostles 19.

wide. But the result was the opposite, for the silt thus hemmed in made the whole harbour as far as the mouth more shallow. Before this time the ebb and flow of the tide would carry away the silt and draw it to the sea outside.'

But whatever steps were taken by man to keep open the ancient Greek ports on the west Anatolian coast, subsequent silting throughout the centuries has proved that the forces of nature predominate.

PART II: SAMOS TO RHODES

Furni Islands
Patmos
Arki
Lipso
Gaidero
Pharmako
Leros
Alinda Bay
Port Laki
Parthani Bay
Kalimnos
Port Kalimnos
Pserimos
Kos
Nisiros
Yali Island
Astipalea (Stampalia)
Maltezana
Scala
Vathy
Panormos
Symi   Iassus
Panormittis   Gümüsslü
Port Symi   Budrom
Kovela   Cape Krio
Skropes Bay   Datcha

Part II: *SAMOS TO RHODES*

(including the Dodecanese and the adjacent Turkish coast)

THE DODECANESE

The 'Twelve Islands' with their mountainous formation, rugged grandeur and indented coastline, make an attractive sailing area for a small yacht.

After being under Turkish rule for many centuries, these islands were ceded to Italy after the First World War and handed back to Greece after the Second.

Sometimes called the Southern Sporades, they appeared to the early Greeks as 'lean wolves'; so close are they to Anatolia that some of their extremities jut into the Turkish gulfs.

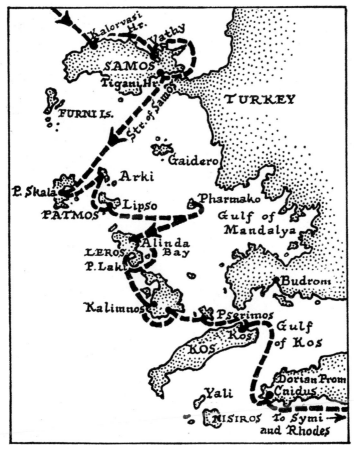

Samos and the Dodecanese

Part of the barren Furni Islands. Showing many inlets, some being pleasant
summer anchorages for small vessels

Kos and Rhodes reflect the recent influence of Italian occupation: the other
islands are sparsely populated but offer some delightful solitary anchorages,
each different from the others in size, shape and character.

The Furni Islands lying between Samos and Patmos are hilly, rocky and
indented. The few inhabitants live on the main island close to the narrow strait;
there are some deserted sandy bays with good shelter—ideal places for anyone
wanting complete isolation.

They were formerly a lair for pirates, one of whose captives, an Englishman named Roberts, writing after his escape in 1692 states: 'They go to Furnes and lie there under the high land hid, having a watch on the hill with a little flag, whereby they make a signal if they see any sail; they slip out and lie athwart the Boak of Samos, and take their prize.'

Today one may walk up this hill and enjoy the same view across the strait towards Samos.

Patmos. Nearing this island from the eastward a vessel passes some rather forbidding rocky spurs, and enters the large sheltered bay; thence a long inlet leads to the Scala, the little port whose buildings, in a modern Italian style, are seen in the distance.

On the hill behind lies the village, dominated by what appears to be a medieval stronghold. It is, in fact, the Monastery of St John the Divine.

Approach and Anchorage. Chart 1669 and 3927. Sailing into the inlet a vessel should make for the modern Italian buildings on the water-front. Anchor in 3 or 4 fathoms northward of a stone pier where the bottom shelves rather steeply. The holding seems adequate and the shelter good, the anchorage being open only to the east. There is also good anchorage at the head of the bay, where it is more sheltered though rather far from the village.

Facilities. A landing in the dinghy may be made near the Customs House, which is convenient for the shops and small restaurants which have recently sprung up in the port.

On account of the monastery and the island's biblical associations, many tourist ships now enter the anchorage for a few hours' stay.

Close to the Customs House, a taxi is available to climb the new well-graded road that spirals up the hill. Half-way is a small monastery built around a grotto, now revered as a shrine, where St John is said to have written the Revelation after having been condemned by the Emperor Domitian in A.D. 96 for preaching the Gospel.

Crowning the hill immediately above the small village is the fortress-like monastery built in the eleventh century—a complicated structure with chapel, treasure room, and library beneath unsymmetrical roofs and bellcotes at different levels. At one time it was full of treasure, some of which, during the last century, found its way to London, Leningrad and Vienna; the most valued asset remaining today is the thirty-three leaves of St Mark's Gospel, written in the fifth century on purple vellum, called the *Codex Porphyrius*. Other treasures are an eleventh-century icon and a more recently carved screen; but in this rich monastery many things are hidden away.

The superb view from the roof of the monastery must not be missed. Looking towards the Anatolian coast the massive mountains of Asia can be seen in the far distance behind the outlying islands of the Dodecanese. An easy walk through the village soon brings one back to the harbour. There is nothing remarkable about the village, but when the French traveller Tournefort came here 200 years ago he expressed surprise at finding twenty women to every man.

Arki lies among a small group of barren islands east of Patmos. It is long and narrow with some attractive sheltered coves and a few fishermen.

> **Approach and Anchorage.** With Chart 3927 this is easy by day, but quite impossible by night.
>
> *Augusta* is the cove recommended by *Sailing Directions*, though the second cove southwards, Port *Stretti*, is probably better from the point of view of depths and swinging room.
>
> The depths shown on chart are inaccurate and in Augusta cove there is 2 fathoms well inside the reach turning northwards, with a sandy bottom in the centre. On anchoring it is wise to take a warp to the shore—perfect shelter from Meltemi.
>
> In the 'port' there are half a dozen fishing boats, some of which fish for crayfish.

About 150 people live on the island in two or three scattered hamlets. Though nothing is produced for export, the people grow enough to live on; an occasional caique runs to Patmos with fish and returns with stores.

Mr Kritikos, the head man of the island, lives in a house between Port Augusta and Port Stretti.

Lipso, lying southward of Arki, is a dull little island with its small port on the S.W. side. The depths behind the new and insignificant breakwater are not enough for a yacht of medium draft to anchor, and outside the holding is bad. Fortunately, farther out and close under the land to the westward, holding is better, though strong gusts from the Meltemi sweeping down the hills, spoil the tranquillity of the anchorage.

The small village adjoining the port is dull and rather poor, though very recently it has been improved with a new quay and concrete roads.

There are two unimportant islands off the Turkish coast:

Gaidero, with a small hamlet at the head of a bay on the south coast, is only 8 miles from Turkey. There are some small sheltered coves here used by a few fishing craft.

Pharmako, lying to the southward, has gentle slopes and is partially covered with green scrub. There are four small coves on the eastern coast, sheltered from the prevailing northerly wind; the north-westerly cove is the most convenient.

Approach and Anchorage. This cove can be recognized by a small white church on the hill above and by four arches of a Roman villa close by the water's edge. The sea bed shelves to a convenient sandy anchorage close offshore in 3 fathoms. Though good in summer, this anchorage is completely exposed to the eastern quadrant.

The island is largely barren with only one small cottage which is lived in today.

Among some Roman remains may be seen the foundations of two or three villas, and underwater there is the rubble of a former jetty; at the southern part of the island there are further remains. Today the only inhabitants are Greek fishermen who spend the summer months here. They keep their boats under the shelter of the loggia of a Roman house, and at night poach the fish from the nearby Turkish coast.

Historical. It was here that Julius Caesar spent many weeks in captivity. In the year 77 B.C. at the age of 22, he was on the way to Rhodes to finish his education when pirates captured him at sea off Miletus and brought him to Pharmako. Here he was kept a prisoner, and a ransom of 22 talents was demanded by the pirates. Meanwhile, Caesar, apparently maintaining an ascendancy over his captors, expressed disgust that his life should be assessed at such a low value, whereupon the pirates raised their price to 50 talents (about £60,000). His many weeks of captivity were well occupied and we are told he wrote poems and speeches, took exercise, and jested with the pirates, assuring them they would eventually be hanged. The ransom from Rome was sent to Miletus and thence to the pirate camp at Pharmako. Caesar, on being released, soon raised a punitive expedition, captured the pirates and had them sent as prisoners to Pergamon, where they were condemned to death by crucifixion.

It is said that, bearing in mind their humane treatment of him during captivity, Caesar had their throats cut before they were nailed to the cross!

Leros, lying south of Lipso is 8 miles long; its many inlets and promontories, afford pleasant summer anchorages. To the north-west of this rugged coast the long island of Arkhangelos forms a shield against the prevailing winds and provides shelter in the remote bays of the Pharios Channel. There are two main ports and some sheltered anchorages:

(*a*) **Alinda Bay.** On the eastern coast is easily distinguished from seaward by the imposing Venetian Castle on the high Punta Castello; the attractive village of Agia Marina lies at the southern side near the head of the Bay which is a minor 'port' for caiques.

Anchorage. Chart 1669. The anchorage is easy to find by day or night. In settled weather a yacht should anchor on a sandy bottom off the town of Agia Marina. If several craft are here it is more convenient to run a warp to the shore close S.W. of the pier with the red light.

Port Facilities. At the shops in the port there is a limited choice of fresh provisions, but at Leros village on the saddle of the hill there are better supplies. There are some fresh-water taps near the quay and one or two modest tavernas. Taxis also are available.

An interesting half-an-hour's drive by taxi from Agia Marina leads up the hill through Leros village and then down to Port Laki. There are fine views across the hilly and unproductive country of the island.

The British cemetery at the head of the bay recalls the determined, though unsuccessful, attempt to wrest this island from the Germans in 1943. Nearly three thousand men were landed at Alinda Bay and the adjoining coves; despite subsequent reinforcing with troops then in Samos, the Germans in the Aegean proved to be too strong. The British had to withdraw, losing many men; six destroyers were sunk and several ships damaged.

(*b*) **Port Laki.** This is the former Italian naval port, and most of the administrative buildings are now in ruins. An attempt has been made to turn the town into a Greek summer resort, but in 1960 it still had a dilapidated appearance.

There are some provision shops, and in the summer plenty of fish. An ice factory lies eastward of the village.

There is also a technical school here and the school for Greek wooden-ship construction.

(*c*) **Parthani Bay.** This is completely landlocked, affording perfect shelter in suitable depths; but the Greek Navy has recently taken it over, and yachts are not encouraged.

Approach and Berth. Chart 3926, and large-scale plan on Chart 1669. There is anchorage with convenient depths of 4 fathoms in the middle, shelving gradually. Some large mooring buoys and other obstructions have been laid out between the entrance to the bay and Porto di Rina, making an approach by night most hazardous.

Kalimnos, view of the port

Kalimnos. A narrow but well-marked strait separates Leros from Kalimnos immediately southward. The beautiful scenery along the west coast of this mountainous and largely barren island should not be missed, and there are some delightful anchorages here, sufficiently sheltered against the prevailing winds.

A windy corner of the Aegean showing summer anchorages
referred to in text

Port Kalimnos is an unattractive though interesting small town with a large artificial harbour. More than half the small houses are colour-washed in blue, said to have been a ruse by the islanders for irritating their former Italian masters by flaunting the Greek colours. The place is unusually dirty for Greece and swarms with noisy children.

Approach and Anchorage. Chart 1669. It is easy to enter, day or night. If the harbour is too congested to swing to an anchor it is advisable to berth with the stern to a stone pier in a depth of 2 fathoms—anchor laid out towards the breakwater. The holding here is poor, and strong gusts during the Meltemi are to be expected.

95

Facilities. There is a limited choice of meat and fresh provisions. There are one or two mediocre tavernas.

Sponge-fishing. The great occupation of the inhabitants for many decades has been sponge-fishing. Several hundred men usually sail during the spring in perhaps eighty boats for the African coast, and base themselves on Tobruk, Bengazi and even Tunis. These small vessels are mostly the local *trehandiri* about 35 feet in length built of Samian pine. This fleet has its own divers with both rubber suits and aqualungs, also sponge fishers with masks for the shallower waters. They are usually to be expected back during October when their return is the occasion for noisy celebrations. Many of their sponges, after local processing, find their way to the American market. During the last War when sponge-fishing was denied them, many men from this island, fearing starvation, escaped in their boats, together with their families, to Turkey.

It is of interest that Kalimnian divers were taken to Kithera in 1802 to assist in retrieving the Elgin marbles, then lying in a wreck in 60 feet of water. (See page 15.)

General. There is a steamer communication with Piraeus and Rhodes at least twice a week, and a caique plies to Kos.

The island can barely sustain its population of nearly fourteen thousand. It was denuded of trees during the long Turkish occupation. Now it grows only a few vegetables, and rears some poor cattle for home consumption.

Other Anchorages. On the east coast there are one or two inlets of which Vathy with a village at its head is interesting: though well sheltered in summer this valley is subject to mountain gusts. In Borio Bay on the west coast is a charming anchorage off a sandy beach lying at the foot of a green valley.

Pserimos is of no particular interest, and its one sheltered cove is on the S.W. coast; this is used by the Greeks as a minor summer resort.

Approach and Anchorage. There is no difficulty by day, but a yacht should beware of a rock awash to the southward of this cove. The sandy bottom in the cove rises conveniently to 3 fathoms, but there is a rocky ledge running across which protrudes about 2 feet above the sand. The Meltemi brings in a lively swell. There are some landing steps on the north side of the cove where tourists from neighbouring islands are landed from caiques.

General. There is a good bathing beach but, apart from a few summer bungalows built close to the shore, no other dwellings can be seen.

Kos. This long barren-looking island has a well-sheltered little port adjoining the white modern buildings of the town.

Approach and Berth. The narrow harbour entrance between the two moleheads is immediately north of the castle. Here there is a minimum depth of $2\frac{1}{4}$ fathoms and not less than 2 in the harbour. Silting of the port: see p. xxii. It can be approached day or night.

Yachts berth with their sterns to the steps at the southern quay with anchors to the northward. Caiques and small steamers also berth here and this quay can be very crowded.

Outside the harbour there is good shelter from the Meltemi close under the east coast in convenient depths on a sandy bottom.

Facilities. Good water may be obtained from a tap by the steps: there is a good market,

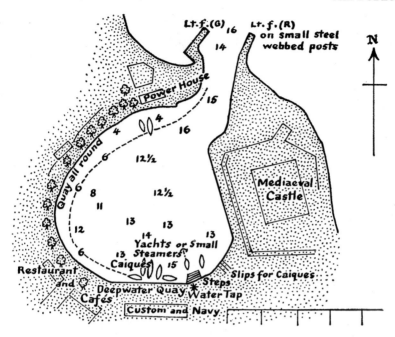

Kos. (*Soundings in feet, from author's soundings and Greek Survey*)

modern shops and three or four restaurants. There are some modest hotels, one having its own bathing beach. Taxis can be hired.

The fast Piraeus-Rhodes steamer stops outside the port, there being a summer service about five days a week. A caique plies to Budrom (Halicarnassus) once a week.

Both town and harbour were reconstructed by the Italians after the earthquake in 1933. Everything of interest adjoins the port: on its N.E. side is the fifteenth-century castle, built by the Knights of Rhodes; the caiques berth off the tamarisk-shaded quays.

The flowering hibiscus and oleanders which border the streets do much towards improving the look of the town with its modern shops, bars and restaurants. One must see the eighteenth-century mosque built of earlier Hellenic and Byzantine columns; the old plane-tree which, according to Hacke writing in 1699, was then 'so vaste that its branches would shade a thousand men'; the local guide explains that Hippocrates used to teach under this tree in the fifth century, but foresters maintain that no plane-tree can live more than five hundred years! The castle of the Knights and an interesting museum should be visited.

Just over two miles outside the town is the Asclepion, the medical school and hospital of Hippocrates, which has been rather over-restored by the Italians. Although its appeal is less than that expected, the view across the Strait towards the Anatolian mountains is magnificent.

Today Kos is a gay little port with plenty of activity; the quays constantly busy with the arrival and departure of caiques, and the daily crowd of jostling passengers being embarked and disembarked by ferry-boats from the mail steamer waiting outside. As far as tourists are concerned Kos might be styled a younger sister of Rhodes.

Historical. When St Paul put in for a night on his third missionary journey, he undoubtedly came to the same harbour as exists today. This silted up in medieval times, but it did not prevent Kos from being used by pirates. A picture of the place two and a half centuries ago under Turkish rule is given by Hacke:*

Here being seven half galleys each carrying three hundred men, forty-eight oars, four guns and everyman's small arms. They also have brigantines each carrying seventy men, twenty-eight oars, six patereroes, and small arms each man. These are governed, owned and commanded chiefly by one man who has his commission from the Grand Senior; and for retaliation he gathers tribute of the Isles yearly, and by which he is no loser, imposing on rich and poor what he pleases and forces them to pay. And in his progress he takes many Christian Slaves.

Anchorage South Side of Kos. Towards the western extremity of the island's south coast is the open Kamara Bay facing towards the S.E. At one time there was a port here and the remains of the early Greek works are still indicated on the chart. This position affords a splendid remote anchorage in northerly gales, and one may land for a walk to the original Hellenic capital which today is marked by a small hamlet.

Nisiros is square-shaped and largely green with two shallow harbours. The land rises towards a ring of hills in the centre, surrounding a depression with volcanic crators. Unlike Milos, the volcanic soil is fertile and there are almond trees on the hillsides. The few small villages are very primitive.

Of the two small harbours, Mandraki is the more important, but in the prevailing Meltemi its short breakwater is insufficient to provide adequate shelter and the bottom is of poor holding and most irregular. In the event of a northerly blow, a vessel should make up for the centre of the small and almost uninhabited Yali Island, lying 3 miles to the north-westward, for here under these conditions both shelter and holding are good.

Astipalea (Stampalia) is the most westerly of the Dodecanese; its twin mountain peaks make it appear in the distance as separate islands. The inhabitants, looking more Turkish than Greek, are poor and number scarcely two thousand; apart from a small export of sheep and honey, they produce barely enough to keep themselves.

* *Collection of Original Voyages*

Of the four natural harbours only Maltezana (with its leading marks and lights) is of any importance. In fine weather vessels usually anchor in the nearby Livardhia Bay, close beside the Scala, it being more convenient for landing passengers and cargo. Should it blow, however, even from the north, the squalls may become too strong to remain, and it is then necessary to shift back to Maltezana. Anchorages are shewn on Chart 3922:

(*a*) **Maltezana.** Provides almost all-round shelter with good holding in most places. (The buoys shewn on the chart, formerly dangerous by night, have been removed.) There is good holding on firm sand in 3 fathoms close westward of the white obelisk.

There are no habitations on the shores, though a road passes close by leading towards the Scala.

(*b*) **Scala.** Though the *Sailing Directions* reflect some doubt as to the safety of this anchorage, the local people claim that even in hard winds (except between south and N.E.) it is considered to be safe. The chart shews a boat harbour, but this is here no longer, nor is there a light exhibited, for the mole does not exist. The short jetty used by fishing craft has about one fathom depth at its extremity. A yacht may anchor in 3 fathoms, 120 yards off.

There is water available from a tap and also from a well 100 yards from the landing. A very small market for fresh produce is nearby, and a bar which may be willing to provide a simple meal. Petrol in limited quantity may be bought from drums.

The Piraeus steamer calls twice a week.

The white houses of the Scala during recent years have been extended up the hill and have joined the Chora, whose Venetian Castle stands on top and is visible for some miles to seaward. Embedded in its outer wall near the gate is a plaque cut with the coat of arms of the Quirini family of Venice, who governed this island for three hundred years until they were overrun by the Turks. A line of windmills painted white and now in a state of disrepair line the ridge between the two villages.

(*c*) **Vathy** is probably the best sheltered and most suitable of the inlets for a yacht though it serves little purpose for the trading caiques.

(*d*) **Panormos** though open to north is claimed to be a good anchorage.

Historical. In Roman days, after the suppression of piracy, warships were stationed at Maltezana to maintain the safety of shipping. Pirates also used these natural shelters in the later centuries, and in 1812 one of H.M. ships having captured a pirate galley reported—

Yet she rowed fast, possessed a swivel and twenty muskets, and with forty ferocious looking villains who manned her might have carried the largest merchant ship in the Mediterranean.

These pirates had just captured a Turkish boat with five men, four of whom were massacred and the fifth, a Jew, had merely been deprived of an ear!

Apart from the rather unusual approaches to these natural harbours, this island hardly merits a special visit.

Symi a rugged, mountainous and largely barren island lies on the eastern extremity of the Aegean within the mouth of the Turkish Gulf of Doris.

It has two harbours: one, Panormittis, on the western side of the island, affording good shelter in depths of 3 fathoms; and the other on the east side, Port Symi, lying in a deep inlet surrounded by colourful little houses.

(a) **Panormittis.** A delightful, enclosed, natural harbour in mountainous surroundings with a monastery by the quay.

Approach and Anchorage. Chart 1604. On the N.E. side of the entrance is a ruined windmill painted white, which stands out conspicuously to the westward at least 5 miles distant. It is reported that a red light is now exhibited there. The shore generally is steep-to.

It is convenient to anchor half way between the S.W. headland of the entrance and the southern extremity of the monastery, in 3 fathoms on a sandy bottom. About 30 yards south of the monastery tower is a short stone pier which also has a quay; at the head of the pier are depths of 8 to 9 feet diminishing towards the shoreward end. Though a yacht could berth with her stern to the pierhead for a short while, it is well to know that caiques frequently call here, as well as the Rhodes steamer.

There is a slight swell caused by the day breeze.

General. Fresh water is limited, being collected in winter and stored in the monastery cistern; there is a small general store in the monastery where tinned provisions and vegetables may be bought; there is also a café.

The rather forbidding modern monastery has a charming bell-tower and, in its courtyard a twelfth-century church, with some interesting carving and icons. Only a few monks live here, but many Greek visitors stay a few days and eat at the café. In front of the monastery is a memorial to the late Abbot who was shot by the Germans in the last war.

The ringing of the monastery bell on the approach of a strange vessel is a sign of welcome and this custom was still continued a few years ago.

(b) **Port Symi,** the capital, is an attractive small town rising in terraces around the head of a mountainous cove.

Approach and Berth. Chart 1669 (plan of Port Symi). There is no difficulty day or night except in N.E. winds, when a swell enters the cove. Owing to the steep gradient of the sea-bed, it is impossible to berth at the side of the creek. A satisfactory berth in convenient depths is to be found at the head of the creek with bows N.E. and stern about 10 yards clear of the quay in 10 feet depth. This is well sheltered from the Meltemi gusts, but rather exposed in event of a strong N.E. wind.

General. Water is scarce, there being only rain water in the private cisterns. Ice can be bought at a factory close by the only (very modest) hotel. The mail boat calls twice a week, berthing at the quay off the clock tower. Vegetables can be bought.

Some thirty years ago Port Symi had a population of seven thousand people, many of whom were employed in the sponge fleet. Today the population is only 2,500 of whom only about fifty men go away sponge-fishing in the summer months.

The yellow colour-washed houses, standing one above the other, rise from the quayside as though in an amphitheatre. Many are mere shells and others deserted, partly the result of war damage, but also due to the general decline of the island's economy. The town is slowly decaying.

On the front wall of one of the houses is a plaque recording in the English and Greek languages the surrender of the Germans in the Dodecanese in 1944.

There is a mule track over the mountains from Port Symi to Panormittis: this passes through a wood of pines and cypresses, but it is rough going and takes at least four hours.

Tilos (formerly Episcopi) is a dull little island with an anchorage in Livardia Bay close to the main village.

Anchorage. Let go in about 7 fathoms off the entrance to the small boat harbour. Here the bottom is sand and the holding believed good. Open to north-east, a swell often comes into the bay.

Facilities. The village, 20 minutes' walk along the shore of the bay, is uninteresting and can provide only limited fresh supplies.

A steamer from Piraeus calls once a week.

There are three villages on the island, whose agriculture has deteriorated, and now the only export is goats. The island has never been of historical importance, but during the period of the Knights its security depended upon warnings of enemy approach which could be signalled to Rhodes from a number of watch-towers—hence the name Episcopi. It has also been said to have derived this Venetian name from having once had a bishop.

THE TURKISH COAST

This section of the Turkish coast is well indented with many sheltered anchorages. Though the distance direct from Samos Strait to Rhodes Channel is only 100 miles, if one cruises inside the three large gulfs of Mandalya, Kos and Doris, it is three times as far. Here are several attractive places still to be explored.

101

Chart 1546 shows clearly a number of inviting anchorages for a yacht in the heads of the inlets of Mandalya Gulf.

Kovela. The present village of Kovela on the eastern shore is poor and squalid, and the shores having silted, there is no longer shelter at the anchorage; it may be used only in settled weather and not in the Meltemi season.

The Turkish Coast. Samos Strait to Rhodes Channel

Formerly the ancient port of Panormos, it handled the commerce of Didyma with which it was linked by a road bordered by sphinxes.

Today there are practically no remains, but it has port officials and is the headquarters of a coastguard detachment: here one may land in fine weather to visit the ruins, not only of Didyma, but also Miletus and Priene, about three hours distant on foot.

North of Kovela is one of the mouths of the Meander River, which, with its broad delta, numerous sharp elbow turns and relatively steep tributary valleys in its higher reaches, is typical of the East Anatolian rivers. The rich alluvial silt perpetually carried towards its mouth has built up an extensive 'flood plain' which having been drained has now become rich agricultural land. Certainly since Greco-Roman days this process has continued, and the present mouth of the river during this period has advanced westward more than 20 miles.

Skropes Bay (Skrophes), a comfortable sandy anchorage and useful for a yacht wishing to visit Didyma.

> **Approach and Anchorage.** Chart 1546. One should give Skrophes shoal a wide berth and approach the anchorage from the E.S.E. This shoal is now only just under the surface and may be seen by the discoloured water. Let go 300 yards to the eastward of the small customs shack in 2½ fathoms, on a sandy bottom. Both holding and shelter are good, the bay being open only to the southward.
>
> **Officials.** There are only the Customs Guards who telephone to the military. Passports are examined, and ships' papers are sent by runner to the authorities in Kovela.

The squalid village of Yeronda is 3 miles distant by a track starting from the Customs-hut, where donkeys may be hired. Beside this village are the extensive remains of the Ionic Temple of Didyma.

> **Historical.** Towering above the village the surviving columns of the temple stand 100 feet above the ground and all around lie the drums of many more where they were felled by the earthquake at the end of the fifteenth century. Though nothing remains of the earlier temple built by Branchus and destroyed by Xerxes after Salamis, these are the ruins of its successor, the vast temple put up by the Milesians. The scale was so grand that even after 150 years' work and despite the subsequent efforts of the Romans, it was still unfinished. Had it been completed it would probably have ranked as one of the Wonders of the World. It was approached by a sacred way from Panormus (now Kovela) lined with statues, of which Newton recovered some seated figures and sphinxes of the sixth century B.C., now to be seen in the British Museum.

After Skropes Bay is **Iassus** with Port Isene, shown in detail, with ancient moles and ruins marked on Commander Graves's early Survey. (Strabo attaches one of the dolphin stories to this place—that of the boy who called it by playing the harp.) On the opposite shore of the inlet is the small poorly sheltered steamer port of Gulluk (or Kulluk) with Turkish Port Authorities whom it is wise to visit before landing.

There are further small and fascinating places along these remote shores of Turkish Anatolia. Few yachts come here, and the only objection to making a cruise to these unspoilt and isolated small coves is the presence of suspicious, armed Customs Guards, often too trigger-happy in their behaviour towards an inoffensive foreign yacht.

Gümüsslü, as the Turks now called Myndus, has little to show beyond the foundations of the old walls.

The harbour entrance is tricky and narrow—during the Meltemi it is almost impossible to enter under sail though the bay is entirely sheltered inside.

The small Turkish hamlet is dull, and since Budrom lies only a few miles to the southward and is of some interest, it is advisable to omit the call at Myndus and visit Budrom instead.

Approach and Anchorage. Though Chart 1604 is not clear, the *Sailing Directions* give a good description. As the 40-yards wide channel of entry reaches its narrowest point, an

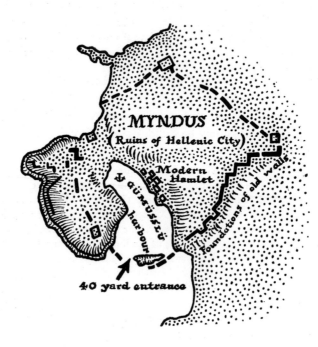

underwater ledge (part of the ancient wall) appears to protrude about 15 yards. The down-blasts from the high promontory during the Meltemi can be disconcerting.

General. Caiques often shelter here when working northwards, off the Turkish coast, in hard northerly winds.

There are only two small cafés and one place to eat.

Budrom is the ancient Halicarnassus and former capital of Caria. Its sheltered port is still protected by the original Greek breakwaters.

The site of one of the famous Wonders of the World—the Tomb of Mausolus—is close beside the harbour on the bare rising ground, but today not a stone remains.

Approach and Berth. Chart 1606 shows the channel between the ancient breakwaters which have recently been built up with a top dressing. The most convenient place to anchor is off the Customs House in 2¼ fathoms, taking care to allow sufficient room to clear the sunken

summit of Thira

ORIN

ing down at the
quay from the
e of Thira 800
bove

Cnidus: entrance to the silted north harbour
showing the deep water harbour beyond

Port Kaio: a deserted harbour in the Mani, the last
resting place of the migrating quail

quays of the 'Secret Port'. The bottom is soft mud with a layer of thin weed and the shelter is good.

Officials. There are the usual quota for a Port of Entry.

General. Though piped water is laid on it is not recommended, and spring water may be bought in carafes. There are two modest restaurants; ice and petrol may be bought.

The only feature of interest here is the castle of the Knights.

Budrom—ancient Halicarnassus. (*Soundings in fathoms*)

The modern Turkish town, mostly built by the former Greek colony, is without interest except on market day when peasants from outlying villages wearing colourful national costume come in by camel with their wares.

The Castle. On the east side of the harbour standing on a rocky eminence are the well-preserved walls of a large medieval castle built by the Knights of St John. During its construction fragments of the Mausoleum were torn down to embellish the castle and some of them remain embedded in the walls today. The English tower with the coats of arms of Plantagenet Knights still stands, despite a hard knock from a British cruiser's bombardment in World War I. Among the scattered pieces of masonry one notices a plinth, a jamb, or an architrave to a doorway, a marble capital lying on its side, carved with an heraldic device.

By far the most important find of Greek sculpture was that of the famous Amazon frieze which, in 1856, Newton,[*] with the British Navy's help, removed from the walls of the castle where the Knights had placed it as decoration. It was carried away by H.M.S. *Siren* together with the 9½-foot statue of Mausolus—'the tall handsome man . . . formidable in War!' Both statue and frieze are well displayed in the British Museum.

The castle was used by the Knights for many years, as a base for making sorties against the Turks, and as a sanctuary for escaping Christian slaves.

[*] C .T. Newton, British archaeologist and at that time appointed British Consul in Smyrna. Some captured Turkish reports described him as the 'mad English Consul digging holes in the ground at Cape Krio'.

Cape Krio, on the end of the Dorian Peninsula, lies conveniently on the route from Kos to Rhodes. This high imposing cape and its adjoining isthmus provide shelter for the two little natural harbours of ancient Cnidus.

The more important one faces south-east and is much used by local craft today. This anchorage is sheltered from the Meltemi by the low narrow isthmus, and from the sirocco by the two ancient moles—'carried to a depth of nearly 100 feet', wrote Captain Beaufort during his survey 150 years ago, 'one of them is almost perfect and the other which is more exposed to the S.W. swell can only be seen under water'.

Approach and Berth. By day this is easy, and a vessel may pass in deep water 20 yards off the extremity of the S.W. mole. Keeping in the centre of the bay, the sea bed rises slowly to 3 fathoms with a bottom of heavy weed on sand. It is extremely difficult to get a plough anchor to hold. Though there is perfect shelter from the sea, strong gusts blow from N.W. by day and from N.N.E. by night during Meltemi periods. Off the Cape itself very violent gusts make it advisable to lower sails before entering harbour.

General. There is an outpost of a dozen Turkish soldiers who usually insist on seeing ship's papers. A crew-list with passport numbers should be prepared to forestall a demand to retain one's passport.

All round the harbour are the terraced walls of large stone blocks rising from the water's edge to the ridge above. Nothing more is visible from the anchorage, but from above can be seen the foundations of the buildings of the ancient city and two Greek theatres. Newton came here in the middle of the last century, and having made a careful survey took away to London a number of relics including the headstone of an Hellenic naval war memorial—a fine 12-ton lion*—the symbol for valour. Another sculpture, one far more famous in its

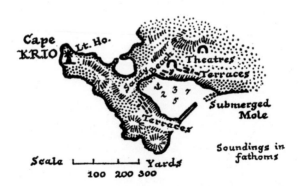

The two small harbours of ancient Cnidus

* He now peers sadly through the gloomy vaults of the British Museum.

Voyage of St Paul on his 3rd Missionary Journey

day, was the beautiful Aphrodite by Praxitiles—removed in the fourth century and taken to Constantinople; it survived for a thousand years, only to be destroyed by fire after the Turks had entered the city. Fortunately copies have remained in existence.

This 'former station for twenty vessels', as Strabo wrote, is worth a visit. If the local Turkish guard can be persuaded to allow one to land, the walk among the ruins to the top of the surrounding hills is an interesting excursion.

Datcha, a few miles inside the gulf, also provides some shelter. It is sometimes easier here to obtain permission to land.

There are other attractive bays and small inlets on the Turkish coast inside these large gulfs.

Although the coast of Caria is mostly barren, the hinterland is not, and as one approaches eastward the shores become greener and more attractive.

> *The face of places, and their forms, decay;*
> *And that is solid earth that once was sea;*
> *Seas in their turn retreating from the shore,*
> *Make solid land where ocean was before.*
>
> DRYDEN, trans. of Ovid's *Metamorphoses XV*

Some Historical Notes on the Turkish Coast. Sailing southwards from Samos there is a choice of routes, passing either among the Dodecanese islands, or proceeding more directly, close by the Turkish coast as St Paul did in A.D. 56, though since his day part of this coast has altered considerably.

He had been in Macedonia and had crossed by sea to Troy, where after walking to Assos he re-embarked for the voyage to the Levant. This was at the time of the Spring equinox; and as St Paul had left barely sufficient time to reach Jerusalem for the celebration of Pentecost, he had to hurry. Probably

Sketch showing the coastline of Gulf of Latmos during the period of Miletus' greatness (about 500 B.C.). 'Miletus once was mighty long ago' (Greek saying)

rowing during the daylight hours, distances of 50 to 60 miles were sometimes made good each day, and at night the vessel was hauled up and the oarsmen rested. From the narrative in Acts 20, it can be calculated that speeds of at least 4 knots were averaged during the longer hops—a performance which can hardly be bettered today by a small modern yacht sailing southwards in prevailing summer conditions, and anchoring at night.

This Anatolian coastline, whose hinterland is sprinkled with ruined cities of the Ionian Greeks and Romans, has seen the greatest change south of Samos where formerly the spacious gulf of Latmos received the outflow of the Meander River. This is now land, and the present coastline many miles to the westward. The ancient gulf once bordered by the large cities of Miletus and Priene had four harbours—'one large enough to accommodate a fleet' as Strabo records. Now all have vanished: 'Furrows take the place of waves, and goats leap where once the dolphins played'. The only part of the gulf still to survive is the inland lake of Bafa: being connected to the sea, a fishing industry has developed, the majority of the fish being cured locally and exported to Greece and to Europe.

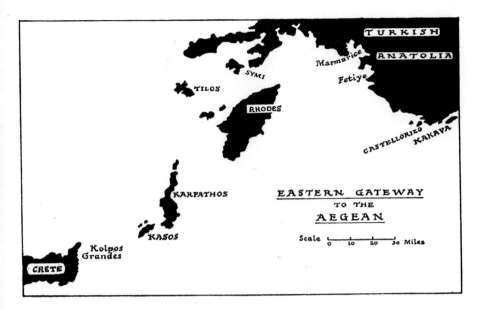

Eastern Gateway to the Aegean

5

The Eastern Gateway to the Aegean

THE ISLAND BRIDGE BETWEEN TURKEY AND CRETE

Rhodes is the largest and most historically interesting island, the capital of the Dodecanese: it is green and mountainous.

By the commercial port the inhabited medieval walled city makes a strange contrast with the large modern tourist resort spreading out from Mandraki.

Mandraki. Chart 1667 with harbour plan.

Approach. Entering the approaches to Mandraki harbour, the extensive medieval walls of the old city come into view as well as the modern pseudo-Venetian buildings close to the quayside.

By day there is no difficulty in the approach. By night, however, if coming from southward along the coast caution is necessary to ensure clearing off-lying shoals.

Berth. Yachts usually berth at the second T-shaped jetty on the western shore, stern to the quay and bows east. The bottom is mud and the water rather foul. (Although completely enclosed and useful as a laying-up port, there can be an uncomfortable surge in the harbour during winter gales from the S.E., when heavy seas sometimes surmount the breakwater.)

Rhodes—Mandraki harbour early Spring. Caiques drying sails after the rain.

A number of caiques from the Aegean use the port, always berthing off the breakwater.
Officials. Health, Customs, Immigration and Harbour Master, this being a Port of Entry.
Port Facilities. Water is laid on by a hydrant near the root of the jetty; its supply and a hose
can be arranged by the Harbour-master. There is petrol and diesel fuel available.

There are plenty of shops close at hand, especially at the white octagonal market. There
are a dozen modern hotels, and several restaurants of various standards. The Bank of Athens
and Ionian Bank have large branches here.

Repairs, both mechanical and skilled artisan, are hard to come by, except in the Old City,
and the two shipyards are only accustomed to ordinary caique shipping and repair work.

A special Customs agreement between the Dodecanese and the Greek Government enables
certain supplies to be bought very cheaply, e.g., petrol, Gordon's gin, hemp and manilla,
excellent tinned meat from Holland and Denmark, biscuits and cosmetics from England, etc.
The best wine is made by C.A.I.R.—excellent red and white, both draft and bottled.

The 20-knot steamers from Piraeus run five times a week (about 20 hours)
and berth at the South Harbour. There is an air service to and from Athens
several times a day; also air communication with Cyprus once a week.

The Town. Rhodes has had many conquerors during its remarkable history. The modern
resort of today was built by the Italians during their domination between the two World
Wars. Not only did they erect the pseudo-Venetian buildings of the new town and lay out
the avenues of flowering trees, but they restored the medieval city. This architecture of the
Knights of St John of the fourteenth and fifteenth centuries is to be seen everywhere in the
Old City, where almost until the First World War the old Turkish custom still continued of
tolling a bell every night at sunset to denote the closing of the city gates. Only Turks and
Jews might then remain within, while visitors from the west had to be content with accommodation provided outside in a little Greek inn.

No one can visit Rhodes without noticing the large stone balls which have
been neatly stacked in piles near the city walls. Many of them are believed to
be the missiles used in the siege of 305 B.C. when Demetrius Poliorcetes of
Syria hurled these monsters from the catapults of his fleet at the city's defences.
As the siege was responsible both for these missiles and for the Colossus, a brief
account extracted from the history by Diodorus Siculus is of interest:

Historical. Known as the Besieger, Demetrius, a claimant to the Empire of Alexander, had
already had success in battle against Ptolemy and Cassander. He wanted to consolidate these
conquests and realized that Rhodes with its great trading fleet lay astride the main sea route
to the Aegean: since it could at any time threaten Demetrius's communications, he decided
to destroy this little 'maritime empire'. A vast expeditionary force of 200 warships and
nearly as many transports was prepared, and with 50 thousand men they set off for Rhodes.

The most remarkable vessels in the expedition were the 'Great Tortoises' or huge monitors,
carrying large catapults and high towers intended to overshoot and destroy the Rhodian
defence towers guarding the moles of the port. The siege was a tough one, and the Rhodians,
although outnumbered held their fortress. Reluctantly forced to withdraw, Demetrius
returned to Antioch and having redesigned his equipment, again returned to the challenge.

This time his new attacking craft was the Helepolis described by Diodorus Siculus as having a large square base and a huge nine-storey tower—higher than any Rhodian watch-tower, and fitted with enormous catapults and drawbridges. Manned by three to four thousand men, it was supported by 'tortoises', and when sighted by the Rhodian look-outs, it must have presented a formidable appearance. This was the master siege-weapon of all times, and it is known that catapults at that period could hurl stones weighing more than half a ton.

The result of the siege depended very much upon the effectiveness of the Helepolis which despite repeated assaults on the harbour and defences, was only partially successful. Meanwhile messages from Syria demanded the immediate return of Demetrius. Reluctantly obeying, he was forced to make terms with the Rhodians; abandoning siege weapons and equipment, he agreed that a colossal war memorial should be built with the proceeds to commemorate this great event. Hence, there came about the erection of the great Colossus cast in bronze and 105 feet high dedicated to Helion, only to be overturned half a century later by the destructive earthquake of 227 B.C.

Afterwards the broken metal lay in the shallow water for nearly nine hundred years, and it was in this state when Pliny, impressed by its immensity, wrote: 'Even lying on the ground it is a marvel. Few people can make their arms meet round the thumb, and the fingers are larger than most statues'.

Now all is gone, the scrap metal, bought by a Levantine Jew, going back to Syria where it was first moulded: but among the piles of huge stone balls still lying by the city walls, some perhaps are the remaining relics of this great siege.

For some centuries local people thought that the great statue stood *astride* the harbour entrance, as shown on the tourist post-cards; but there is no evidence of this from the early descriptions.

The fine medieval walled city built by the Knights of St John more than six centuries ago is largely intact. After they had been driven from Palestine at the end of the thirteenth century, the Knights captured this island from the Byzantines and soon began to build their city. With the support of the Venetians and the Genoese they were established in a key position to plunder Turkish shipping and exercise control of commerce in Levant waters. The building of fortresses at Halicarnassus, Kos and Castellorizo, helped them in these activities which lasted more or less continuously until 1522, when the Knights, having withstood two sieges from the Turks, finally capitulated. They were however treated with great consideration, being allowed to evacuate the island with their arms and belongings, sailing first for Cyprus and finally after a period in Tripoli, making Malta their ultimate home. The best of the Knights' architecture remaining today is the Street of the Knights, and the fourteenth century hospital, now the museum. Most remarkable too are the very broad walls, more than two miles in length and surrounded by a moat 50 feet deep, hewn from the rock.

On leaving the town, the sight of the green countryside with its pleasant villages soon restores the feeling of being in Greece. Lindos, 20 miles down the S.E. coast, should not be missed, nor should the Hellenic city of Kamiros and the Castro of the Knights on the north-west coast. The scenery, particularly in the southern part of the island, is very fine.

Lindos, one of the three Hellenic cities, lies at the top of a high headland whose sides fall abruptly into the sea. Beneath it is Port Lindos a sheltered summer anchorage from which one may conveniently land to visit the Acropolis.

Approach. See plan on Chart 1667—recently re-surveyed by the Greek Admiralty and now published.

There are no harbour lights, so that except under a bright moon and with previous knowledge, entry by night would be difficult.

Anchorage. Let go in 5 fathoms about the letter 'M' on chart. The nature of the bottom varies, being in some places mud or sand on flat rock and occasional ridges of weed which would afford poor holding. There is good shelter except between E. and S.E.

Port Facilities. A path leads up to the village which has a small hotel and restaurant, and a few provision shops. There is daily bus communication with Rhodes.

Lindos makes a pleasant day's sail from the town of Rhodes and back during the Meltemi season when there should be a broad reach and smooth water both ways. The Acropolis of Lindos, set on a rock high above the sea, is one of the most spectacular sites in Greece. Here is evidence of the whole history of the island, more dramatically and lucidly displayed than at any similar site in Greece. There is the classical Greek colonnade which caps the high platform of the Acropolis with the temple of Athena Lindos, the ruined Byzantine church and the castle of the Knights. Even the Turks have left a fortification to round off this long tale of history.

Beneath it is the modern village where it is pleasant to wander among the little white houses. Lindos was once famous for its pottery, and a few old pieces can still be seen in some of the houses.

The walk to Cleobolus's tomb is well worth it for the view of the Acropolis and the bay.

Other Anchorages. *Sailing Directions* refer to a number of places in open bays off this coast suitable according to the weather. The south-east coast of Rhodes, which is mostly steep and hilly, provides several sheltered anchorages under a good lee during summer conditions.

When leaving Rhodes to cross to Karpathos and Crete it may be necessary to anchor and wait for the weather to moderate. There are two convenient coves with excellent shelter and holding close to the southern Cape of Nosos, where a vessel can await the opportunity for crossing. It is also necessary to bear in mind the impeding short sea that is sometimes whipped up over the shallow bank extending south-westward from the extremity of Rhodes.

Outlying Islands. A few miles off the N.W. coast of Rhodes are two outlying islands Alimnia and Khalki. Though of little interest themselves, it is worth sailing from Mandraki to Alimnia for the view of the castles of the Knights perched in prominent positions on the Rhodian coast.

(*a*) **Alimnia** has a well-sheltered bay rather deep for anchoring. In unsettled weather there is a choice of two convenient coves where, with a warp ashore, a small vessel can lie safely in a hard blow from any direction.

Approach. Chart 1667. There is no difficulty by day, though it would not be advisable to enter at night.

Berth. At the head of the bay a slight lee is provided by the remains of a breakwater extending from a small projection of the shore on which is built a small church.

In a southerly gale the caiques, seeking shelter, prefer to anchor in the small square bay, the south-east corner of the harbour, but the bottom shelves steeply and one should be prepared for a shift of wind.

General. Although the castle is in ruins, the view from the hill-top is magnificent. Only twenty-five people live in this little hamlet and they communicate with Rhodes by caique, landing sometimes at Castella.

(*b*) **Khalki.** The partially sheltered Emporio Bay has a crumbling village at the water's edge and a medieval castle on the mountain behind.

Approach and Berth. Chart 872. The off-lying islands make the approach hazardous by night.

Berth off the quay by the centre of the village with a stern warp ashore. This is not a

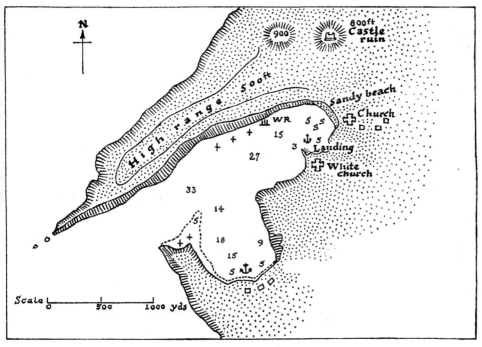

Alimnia: best anchorage in southerly gales. Very steep rising sea bed. (*Soundings in fathoms.*)

desirable place to bring up except in very settled weather. A mooring buoy is provided for the use of small steamers, the holding being poor.

The Castle of the Knights lies in a dramatic setting on a peak nearby, 2,000 feet up behind the village.

The houses of this village recently appeared to be in a state of disrepair and largely empty. Agriculture seemed to be mostly abandoned, though on the island there was still a population of over 3,000. Communication is maintained with the main island of Rhodes by caique which runs daily to Longonia on the opposite coast.

Karpathos (Scarpanto) forms with Kasos the bridge between Rhodes and Crete: Karpathos, long, mountainous and narrow, and Kasos small and insignificant. Neither has an adequately sheltered harbour suitable in the summer months.

Karpathos's one sheltered harbour Tristoma is closed all the summer and autumn months because of the dangerous sea breaking at its mouth; the only port of call then is Pegadia on the south-eastern shore.

The tall mountain range forming the spine of the island runs from end to end and causes hard gusts to sweep down to the shores along the S.E. coast. Hence there are only a few places where landing is possible: in addition to Pegadia and some small sandy bays at the S.W. end of the island, there is a landing place at Palatia on the little island of Saria.

General Information. There is a number of small villages scattered around on the mountain slopes, but the island produces hardly any exports.

One of the few reasons for visiting Karpathos is to see the interesting national dress worn by the women in the north of the island. Long boots and white breeches; then a long white skirt which is looped up when working, in a similar manner to that adopted by the Dalmatian women at Zlarin in Yugoslavia. They may be seen in the fields any day of the week wearing this picturesque costume.

(*a*) **Pegadia,** the principal village of the island, has recently had some quays and a shore mole constructed and is now known as Port Karpathos.

Approach and Anchorage. Chart 2824 shows the anchorage. A new and very short mole running in a westerly direction from a small projection the north side of the town provides inadequate shelter.

Lay out an anchor and secure stern either to foreshore (with a long warp); or to the breakwater, provided there is no strong Meltemi. Depths are about 4 fathoms nearly half way along the mole, and the bottom is mud. Shelter is poor and there is often a swell. It is sometimes preferable to anchor in the northern corner of the bay as suggested in *Sailing Directions*.
Facilities. There are a few provision shops and there is spring water in some of the houses. No restaurant or hotel; one or two tavernas. The mail boat calls twice a week.

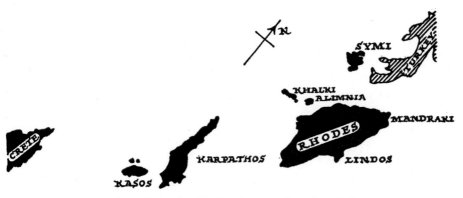

Rhodes and the Island Bridge between Anatolia and Crete

Only a few hundred people live in the village around the port, some of whom are employed fishing.

Note. British charts sometimes mark Karpathos as Scarpanto.

(*b*) **Tristoma** is an attractive and out-of-the-way harbour with half a dozen houses, 3 hours by mule from nearest village. It cannot be used during the Meltemi season or during strong onshore winds.

Approach and Anchorage. The plan on chart 2824 gives detailed information.

In offshore winds very strong squalls blow out of the harbour between South Islet and Tristoma bluff, making entrance under sail impossible. *Note:* (*a*) the ruined church shown on chart, north of Church point, no longer exists; (*b*) a flashing light has been established on South Islet.

Anchor as suggested in Admiralty plan on chart 2824, bearing in mind the possibility of strong squalls.

Facilities. There are no shops, but small quantities of bread, meat and flour may be bought locally.

Other Anchorages on Karpathos. The only good lee during strong N.W. winds appears to be in a sandy bay near the southern tip of the island; this is much used by small vessels on passage to Crete.

Kasos, the mountainous and barren-looking little island lying between Karpathos and Crete, has half a dozen hamlets but no harbour. A small amount of agricultural produce is got away from Rhodes by the mail-steamer which during fine weather anchors off Ofris on the north side of the island. Here boats communicate with this small village at the head of an open bay, entirely exposed to north.

When caught in bad weather caiques use an anchorage under the lee of the islets north of Kasos where there is good shelter in convenient depths on a sandy bottom. The low lying islet of Makronisi is claimed to be the best choice.

The Kasos Strait between Kasos and Crete is 25 miles across, and is frequented by Levant and coastal traffic. If seeking shelter under the east coast of Crete, the safest anchorage to make for is Kolpos Grandes—see Chart 1555. Though open to E., Daskalia anchorage or those recommended by *Sailing Directions* are safer to approach than Sidero Cove (Ayios Ioannis) which should only be attempted by day and during calm weather. (See chapter 6: Crete.)

THE ANATOLIAN COAST FROM RHODES CHANNEL AS FAR AS KAKAVA ROADS

This was part of the former kingdom of Lycia, and from the root of the Dorian promontory continuing on past Marmarice towards the foothills of the Taurus, the nature of the coast becomes more attractive. The great forests stand out against a background of tall mountains whose sharpness of form is unequalled anywhere in the Mediterranean.

This coast was first accurately shown on the charts at the beginning of the last century when Captain Beaufort, hydrographer and archaeologist, moved along the shores and into the hinterland, recording, surveying, and identifying

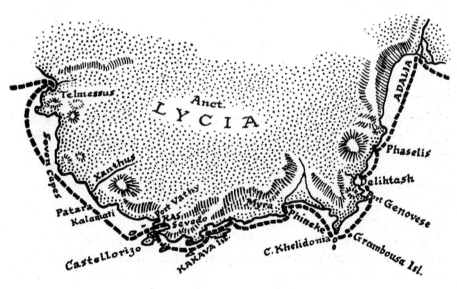

The shores of Karamania (Asia Minor)

AEGEAN LANDMARKS

In the north: Prosphori tower

In the south: the tower at Methoni

Southern Anatolia: a Lycian 'riviera', Kakava Roads

all he saw. It was not always easy to determine the setting of each ruined site, for names had changed throughout the centuries, and the illiterate Turks whose tribes had been settled near these places since the twelfth century had no knowledge to impart. Only by a study of the classical writers and the reading of such Greek inscriptions as were found, could these sites be identified and accurately located on the modern maps and charts.

When crossing from Rhodes harbour to the Turkish mainland, the nearest small anchorage is the old Rhodian settlement of Loryma on the coast immediately opposite. In Port **Aplotheka**, a yacht can moor close inshore in depths of 2 to 3 fathoms well sheltered from the Meltemi.

Proceeding north-eastwards a visit should be made to places in the three large bays, especially to

Marmarice, a delightful, green, mountainous fjord with several coves, but an uninteresting little town at its head.

> **Approach and Anchorage.** Chart 1545 shows all details. The anchorage off the town pier is exposed and for a small yacht there is only slight protection. Squalls from the mountains are to be expected. No lights are exhibited at night.
>
> **Other Anchorages.** Kumlu Buko and the cove immediately north are delightful anchorages. Better still is the cove in the southern corner of Turune Buku (thick weed on sand); it is the best sheltered.
>
> **Officials.** This is a Port of Entry, with Immigration, Health, Police, Customs and Harbour officials.
>
> **Facilities.** Marmarice is a poor little town and has little to offer except some fresh provisions; there is no ice.

In the early part of the century this bay was visited annually by British and Austrian fleets, but nowadays though a few yachts and the occasional Greek caique or small steamer visit the port, it seems to show no progress. Its green mountainous surroundings, however, are very beautiful, and this attractive coast should be followed eastwards.

Karangac Harbour (ancient Cresse). A large inlet lies eastwards with a good sheltered anchorage in Uruk Cove, though rather deep for a yacht.

Keugezi Bay has a less sheltered but deep anchorage in Ekinjik Limani. By the eastern entrance to the bay is the Keugezi river which in Strabo's time permitted ships to berth at its port of Caunus. Its ruins are now $2\frac{1}{4}$ miles from the coast, the walls of the old city and rock towers being visible from seaward.

> **Approach.** The river entrance, only 100 yards wide and shallow, can be identified by red-coloured rock at the western entrance.

Anchorage is off the islet, on sand in 3 fathoms: rather exposed. The river is not navigable by dinghy as the seaward end is largely a swamp.

Rounding the tall Disi Bilmez cape (1,340 feet) 7 miles S. one soon comes to Papas Island (crowned by a brick tomb pyramid), behind which is a suitable anchorage off some ruins on the low-lying mainland. 1½ miles N.E. the fast flowing Ialamon river from the Western Taurus debouches into the sea.

Ten miles S.E. is Cape Kurt which opens into the Gulf of Fetiye with the main port of that name lying in the eastern corner.

Skopea Bay on the western side with a number of remote islands and creeks affords interesting wild surroundings and good shelter for a yacht. On the north of Tersaneh island is a village, standing among the ruins, with a small sheltered port.

Fetiye is a small commercial port adjoining some chrome mines with an uninteresting town of eight thousand people. It lies in the heart of a steep mountainous setting with very green valleys ascending the foothills of the Taurus ranges.

Approach. Chart 1886 with harbour plan (not essential) and *Sailing Directions* makes the approach easy. When nearing the quay a vessel should pass to the westward of a lighted buoy marking the extremity of a shoal protruding from the eastern side of the bay.

Anchorage. A yacht may anchor either off the Customs House in 5 fathoms, or lay out an anchor to the northward and haul in her stern to the quay (ringbolts are fitted). The holding is firm sand.

Officials. Health, Customs, Police and Harbour-master.

Port Facilities. Though water is laid on both to a tap and a hydrant, its purity is doubtful, and it is often in short supply. A new pipeline was being laid in 1955.

There are a few fresh provision shops; one or two simple restaurants; ice and petrol may be bought.

General. A number of men work in the chrome mines on the eastern side of the inlet. The ore is brought in by lorry to the oreships—up to 10,000 tons, which anchor off.

A new quay, 250 yards in length, was being constructed in 1955 with depths up to 5 metres alongside. The various port offices are rebuilt by the quay, and it is intended that ore vessels should berth in future with a stern hawser to the new quay.

More than a century ago Fetiye was a port of call for 'government expresses and travellers from Constantinople embarking for Egypt'. Small British warships, brigs or sloops, sometimes put in for shelter, their captains complaining of the ill effects of 'this mean little port on the men's health'. On board the *Tigre* with Sir Sidney Smith, 100 of his crew were sick. Malaria was then the great scourge.

SYRIAN SCHOONER

HULL AND SAIL PLAN

Approx Scale 0   10   25   50 *feet*

HOVE DOWN FOR REPAIRS

All were built at Ruad but are now only repaired there. They are only to be seen in the waters of Syria, Lebanon, Egypt, Southern Anatolia and Cyprus. Nowadays their jib-booms have all been removed and the long main boom shortened.

Though the town has been greatly improved in recent years with modern drainage and electricity, it is still a dull place with very limited amenities.

Of the ancient Telmessus, there now survive only a few rock tombs. In the last 150 years most of the ancient remains have been quarried for modern building—even the theatre can scarcely be traced.

Lycian tombs, which are remarkable at several places along this coast, are also to be seen here. On a steep cliff-face above the town are three Lycian tombs still in a reasonable state of preservation. The most interesting, with its classical facade, has two well-proportioned columns and drooping Ionic capitals supporting an ample entablature. There are stone panels on the face of these tombs, which have long since been broken into and robbed. This early Christian violation of tombs was undoubtedly stimulated by Theodoric, the Gothic king who, believing so much treasure to be locked up in tombs, proclaimed it the duty of all men to set it free by desecrating the dead. With regard to statuary the Mohammedan considered all imitation of the human figure to be impious, and the admiration of them idolatrous.

The rock into which these tombs were cut is impregnated with iron and in the course of time the stone has 'wept'. In the evening light the whole cliff-face assumes a golden tint with veins of red and brown.

From the viewpoint on the cliff the green Makri valley can be seen receding into the hills with its forests and lush vegetation.

Trade in Syrian Schooners. The Valona oak forests on the plain, and also the pine woods have been sources of supply for Egypt throughout the centuries. This is largely shipped in Syrian schooners, distinctive Bermudian rigged vessels which, despite having no cross-trees, have reasonably lofty masts with lengthy bowsprit and jib-boom. Their origin is obscure. All are built at Ruad, an island off the Syrian coast; usually about 70 feet on the water-line, they have a clipper-bow. They are crewed by four or five Syrian Arabs who live in the height of discomfort.

Though all these schooners are now fitted with engines, they still seize the opportunity of setting their sails in the more gentle winds off the Levant coast. A hard wind would un-doubtedly part their rigging and blow the canvas to ribbons, for their sailing gear is invariably in an appalling condition.

Gemili Island, lying close off the peninsula south of Fetiye, affords a charming anchorage in a small cove on the north side of the island.

Patara. Continuing southward past the Seven Capes the ruins of the old Lycian Capital Xanthus lie inland, but the mouth of the Xanthus River and the ancient port of Patara are still in evidence on the coast. From seaward the ruins of a theatre and some Greek columns can be seen; and in calm weather it is easy to land on the sandy beach. To the southward are huge piles of sand blown up by winter gales in the course of centuries, and to seaward half a mile off shore are whirls of dirty sandy water, evidently from the Xanthus River forced up under pressure from the seabed.

It was at Patara where St Paul, having made a fast passage down the Aegean in A.D. 55 'found a ship crossing to Phoenicia, went on board and set sail'.

Castellorizo, an outpost of Greece close off the Turkish Anatolian coast, is a scorched, barren little island with a decaying port, which affords good protection for a yacht.

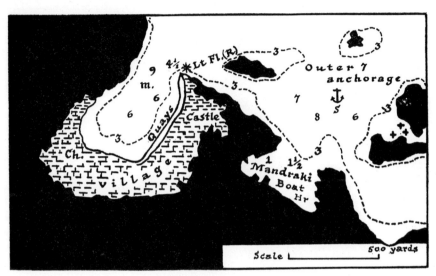

Castellorizo. (*Soundings in fathoms*)

Approach. Chart 2188. On entering the port, anchor as convenient and haul in the stern to the quay.
Port Facilities. At the rather bare café, ouzo and a little wine may be obtained, but food is poor; only goat's meat and unappetising fish can be provided. Fresh water is very limited, and is collected in private cisterns.

Although it has an appeal, the little town, tucked under the eastern arm of the bay, is largely uninhabited. Damaged by fire during British occupation in the last war, the lack of trade has driven away the inhabitants.

Formerly Castel Rosso of the Genoese, it is known as Meis by the Turks today. Before the 1914–18 war, when part of Turkey, this small island had a population of nearly twenty thousand Greeks and at one time its trade was of sufficient importance to merit more than one European consul. Only six hundred people live here today and many of them are looking forward to emigrating to the States and Australia.

On the hill overlooking the harbour is the ample white church with Corinthian columns brought in some past century from an ancient Greek temple at Patara. Close to the church is a Greek school, also far too large for present requirements; both these buildings now strike one as a reminder of the island's more prosperous days.

There are still some ruins of a fortress on the summit, probably erected originally by the Knights of St John who held the island until 1440.

Until the last century Castellorizo was an important pilot station, for many vessels were then in the firewood trade with Egyptian and Syrian ports, and others sometimes put in for provisions and water.

Castellorizo's only connection with the outside world is now maintained by the steamer which plies weekly from Rhodes. This 56-mile voyage is her lifeline, yet within hailing distance are the green shores of Turkey with its richly timbered hinterland which until recent years provided such valuable commerce for both Greek and Turk alike.

Kas. A simple little village with a small harbour formed by its ancient Greek mole lies in a mountainous setting.

> **Approach.** Though no mention is made of this place either on the chart or in *Sailing Directions*, it is of some interest. The place may be recognized by the cluster of white houses forming the small village, and by the Greek theatre on the hill to the northward. The harbour entrance is difficult to discern until one is close to, because the ancient mole is partially submerged. The entrance is about 60 yards wide and there is a depth of at least 6 fathoms until close to the centre of the harbour.
>
> **Berth.** Let go in 4 fathoms where there is a patch of sand. There is just room to swing. Shelter is relatively good, and some of the small craft lie here all the year round; they tuck into the N.W. corner of the harbour.
>
> **Officials.** A Port of Entry. Health, Customs, Police and Harbour-master.
>
> **Port Facilities.** There are some landing steps, yet nowhere to leave a dinghy. Though some fruit may be bought in the market, there are no provisions shops. There is no restaurant, neither is ice obtainable. Fresh water is piped from a mountain stream, but people complain of the calcium.

Kas is a poor little village of a thousand people, formerly called Andiphilo. An occasional steamer on the Istanbul-Iskanderoon service calls for passengers, and except in winter there is road communication with Fetiye and other coastal places. There is a small export of Valona oak by caique, and sometimes a schooner collects cedar wood for Egypt.

There is a very well-preserved Greek theatre with 26 rows of seats facing southward and affording a fine view over the fjords; a number of Lycian tombs outside the village, as well as others, now largely destroyed, stand on the cliff above. From the northern side of this ridge there is a commanding view of the long sheltered fjord, Port Vathy.

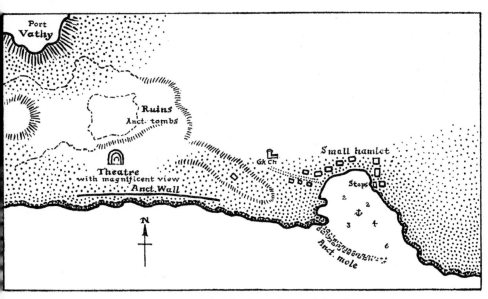

Kas, ancient Andiphilo. (*Soundings in fathoms*)

Though today this Greek-like village has a decayed look, it was a flourishing port until its separation from Castellorizo during the Turco-Italian war early in the century. At that time cedarwood from the interior and firewood were major exports.

Port Vathy is a long steep-to gulf with a sandy shore at its head. Here occasional Turkish caiques bring up to the beach to load their cargoes.

The depths are too great to provide suitable anchorage for a yacht, but larger vessels sometimes make use of the shelter. In the Second World War British destroyers used this anchorage for operations against the German-held Castellorizo.

Port Sevedo. A spacious and completely deserted bay with high steep-to cliffs, excellent shelter; but very deep—a useful undisturbed anchorage.

Approach. Chart 236 and *Sailing Directions* are all that are necessary for a daylight approach. The ledge which extends underwater from the northern point of the entrance was evidently a substantial breakwater in the early nineteenth century, and Beaufort describes it as suitable for 'heaving down ships of the line'.

Anchorage. There is 5 to 6 fathoms in the S.E. corner of the bay with barely room to swing. It is well to run a warp from the stern to the rocks. The holding is mud, and the shelter from southerly and westerly winds is good—a slight swell enters.

The tall brown cliffs, honeycombed with Lycian tombs, look very fine in the evening light. There is no visible habitation in the bay, though there are a few farmhouses not far away. Wild boar sometimes come down at night seeking water by the dried-up torrent.

Kakava. One of the most fascinating and spectacular parts of the south Turkish coast.

Approach. Chart 236 shows the suitable places, which are easy to approach by day, but not possible at night.

The rocks on either side of the S.W. entrance to Kakava Roadstead (the 'unusual entrance' of *Sailing Directions*) and the two islets either side of Tristomos, are marked by white flashes of paint.

The whole district is known as Kakava. The following observations are made on the three anchorages:

(*a*) **Kakava Roadstead.** Xera Cove by the ruined church is probably better than the anchorage on the north side of the roadstead, one mile east of the castle. Here the bottom is considerably deeper than that charted, there being one position with 11 fathoms on the 5-fathom contour line. There is barely room to anchor here in 5 fathoms and a line must be run ashore to the rocks. A few small local boats berth here, and the place is very cramped.

The castle and Lycian tombs only a few minutes' walk away should certainly be explored.

(*b*) **Tristomos** is well sheltered but dull; there is a small village on its northern shore.

(*c*) **Yali Bay** is charming. It is well sheltered and completely deserted. A track leads up to the ruins of ancient Myra where from its now silted port St Paul embarked in a Roman corn ship on his last voyage to the westward.

Early in the nineteenth century Beaufort described many ruins on Kakava island and these are shown on the chart; but today little remains except the sides of cisterns* hewn from the rock, and a Christian church partially destroyed. On the mainland, standing boldly on the high rocky slope, and commanding the western entrance to this long fjord as well as to Tristomos, is an imposing fortress partly of Turkish construction, though probably of Genoese origin. Its isolated dignity is impaired only by the rambling Turkish hovels which ascend from the water's edge as far as the castle ramparts.

Of greatest antiquity are the Lycian tombs—the sarcophagus type, perhaps of Alexander the Great's period—which when viewed from seaward appear on the skyline like recumbent monsters and look quite grotesque among their barren surroundings. All have been plundered long ago, one panel in each having been chipped out of its mullioned frames. After scrambling ashore on a summer's day to enjoy the spectacular view from the fortress across the fjords, a glaring hot sun reveals under the clear blue water more than one tomb already well covered by the sea.

* His ship used to replenish her tanks from these cisterns.

Other than the sarcophagi, no ruins are visible on the mainland today, yet it seems not unlikely that before the soil eroded away and the main coastal road was destroyed, the whole area might have been one great Riviera.

And when we had sailed over the sea of Cilicia
and Pamphylia, we came to Myra, a City of Lycia.
ACTS OF THE APOSTLES

Myra. From Yali Bay a goat-track leads up to Myra, whose ruins can be seen on the foothill a few miles to the north-east, and beneath it, farther along the coast, was the port where St Paul trans-shipped on his last voyage for trial in Rome. Of the port itself nothing but the walls of a granary remain, for the sand has spread along the old river mouth and stopped its egress into the sea; but the silt appears to have built up a rich agricultural plain between the shore and the rising ground where many peasants may be seen working on the land.

St Nicholas. Proceeding by the track it is a rough walk to Myra, which apart from its ruined temples and tombs was famous for its bishop, Nicholas; after his persecution by the Emperor Diocletian, he was later canonized, becoming the patron saint of sailors, virgins, pawn-brokers and children, and in more modern times of Russia. Most of his bones were carried off to Bari in the eleventh century and, shortly after, some more were taken to Venice; the Russians during the last century claimed to have collected what was left, and taken them in a frigate to St Petersburg. Now the Turks, not wishing to disappoint tourists who visit Antalya (a port farther eastward along this coast), have provided even more relics of the saint in their local museum. In England nearly three hundred churches are dedicated to St Nicholas, who is sometimes portrayed with three boys in a tub: these he had miraculously restored to life after they had been murdered and concealed in a vat of brine by a wicked inn-keeper of Myra. The other story concerns the three virgin daughters of an impoverished citizen who, having failed to procure fit marriages for them, was on the point of giving them up to a life of prostitution when the bishop intervened by anonymously presenting each with a bag of gold. The legend spread, and the custom of giving presents in secret attached itself to Christmas day; 'Santa Claus' is merely an American corruption from the Dutch 'San Nicolaas'.

Though there are a number of sheltered places still farther east along the coast of Pamphylia, it is felt they are beyond the actual 'Approaches' to the Aegean.

Local Winds off Karamania. The Meltemi, which blows so hard from the west in the Rhodes channel, is lifted by the Taurus Mountains and seldom reaches the Karamanian coast. East of Fetiye light sea breezes are usually experienced.

THE NORTH COAST OF CRETE

6

The North Coast of Crete

Cnossus, her capital of high command;
Where sceptred Minos with impartial hand
Divided right;

ODYSSEY XIX

Known as Kriti to the Greeks, this large island was once the centre of the western world and the home of the first European civilization.

It is Greece's longest and tallest island, being 140 miles in length: Mount Ida is in the centre of the great chain of high mountains rising to more than 8,000 feet.

Rich finds of the early Minoan and Mycenean civilization are admirably displayed at Heraklion, Knossos and Phaestos etc. The medieval architecture still surviving is Venetian, and the houses and streets of the larger towns are the legacy of the Turks. They held the island for two and a half centuries, having wrested it from the Venetians after the 20-year siege of Heraklion in 1669, and they ruled it until the Greco-Turkish war, when in 1912 Crete was handed back to Greece. Since then some good roads have been built and the towns have been improved with a few modern hotels and houses.

The country scenery is grand; although more than half the island is impossible to cultivate, the northern slopes of the mountains and the elevated plains are rich with vines, olives and farm produce. There are areas of forests, but no rivers, the rain water running away in torrents.

The half-million inhabitants who live in the villages and small towns, mainly on the northern coast, differ from the mainland Greeks. Though St Paul complains of their being 'always liars, evil beasts, slow bellies', these people today are certainly in a different category and though very independent by nature are pleasant enough to strangers visiting Crete.

The Winds off Northern Crete. During the summer months north-westerly winds may be expected generally.

From the eastern end of Crete as far as Heraklion winds are almost invariably N.W., but in the Souda Bay–Chania area they become north; and in the Kithera Channel westerlies predominate with periods of N.E.

Although the northern shores are open to the prevailing wind, all the summer there is sufficient shelter for a yacht at most of the ports listed.

O father Jove, who rul'st on Ida's height most great, most glorious!
ILIAD XXIV

The Ascent of Mount Ida (Psiloritis) about 8,100 feet can easily be made in a pleasant three-day expedition.

There are four alternative routes, each with a place convenient to spend a night during either the ascent or descent: there are

Anoyeia   33 kilometres from Heraklion
Gergeri   39 kilometres from Heraklion
Voutsari   41 kilometres from Rethimnon
Kamares   53 kilometres from Heraklion

All these can be reached by bus.

If one chooses the Kamares route a bed may be found there before starting off with a guide (about £3) next morning. A visit should be made to Kamares Cave where the famous Minoan pottery, named after it, was recovered and sent to Heraklion. From the cave to the western summit takes about five hours. On the summit is the little Stavros church, where a night can be spent.

Descending the following day, the Nidha plateau (3,300 feet) can be reached in three hours and if desired the night may be spent here with the shepherds: food must be taken, and it is useful when setting off to carry also a supply of cigarettes and sweets—gifts for men and children—for those people living all summer in high altitudes are completely cut off.

From the Nidha plateau the Idean Cave where Minoan pottery was also discovered should be visited, and from there the descent to Anoyeia takes about five hours.

Sidero* or **Ayios Ioannis** (on Admiralty charts) is a minute 2-fathom cove close under Cape Sidero affording shelter in all weather except S.E.

Approach and Anchorage. Chart 2536 B is on too small a scale and the plan on 1555 is better. 'Wreck rock' is most dangerous as it protrudes only one or two feet above water and is difficult to see. In event of bad weather Daskalia cove would be easier to make; both anchorages should be approached in daylight only.

The bottom, of firm sand, has a constant depth of 2 fathoms when inside, but there is not room to swing. Moor fore-and-aft, S.E.–N.W.

There are no facilities of any kind, the only inhabitants being the crew of four for the light-house, and a fisherman with his family.

Sitia is a small town with a protecting mole—of no particular interest except that an excursion can be made from there by car to the old monastery of Toplou.

Approach and Anchorage. Chart 2536 B is sufficient to find the anchorage. A broad stone mole with a quay running about E.S.E., a distance of about 70 yards, has now been constructed. Its root is slightly southward of the Venetian castle and at its extremity is a fixed (red) light.

* On the latest chart (1962) the name has been omitted altogether.

Here are depths of 17 feet for some 20 yards inshore, after which they decrease rapidly; if preferring to anchor off, there are suitable steps at the quay to land by dinghy.

Port Facilities. Fresh provisions and ice can be obtained at shops on the quay. Water by tap at the root of the mole. Bus services ply to neighbouring villages and to St Nikolo. There are two small hotels and a modest restaurant and cafés.

The town's population has recently increased to five thousand people, owing to the development of the farming country in the neighbouring valley.

St Nikolo (Ayios Nicolaos). A little fishing port with a protecting mole. Useful to a yacht if visiting the ancient sites.

Approach. Chart 1555 (plan). A mole has been constructed since the War from the N.W. eminence of Mandraki Pt. It runs in a direction W.N.W. and then N.W. for nearly 100 yards. It is marked by a red flashing light at its extremity. There are depths of 5 fathoms at the entrance and deep water all along. Yachts are advised to berth near the ramp at the root of the mole.

Shelter, during a strong Meltemi, is inadequate in the harbour, and vessels generally move across to Nikolo Point, where the lee is excellent.

Officials. This is a Port of Entry with the usual authorities.

Facilities. St Nikolo is the capital of Lassithi province, and has banks, hospital, etc. Water, though laid on to the quay, is not always available; but it may be bought from a lorry at a cost of about fifteen shillings for 2 tons. There are one or two restaurants, cafés, and hotels.

A car may be hired to drive to the Minoan town of Gurnia, the Byzantine church at Kritsa, and the monastery of Faneromeni.

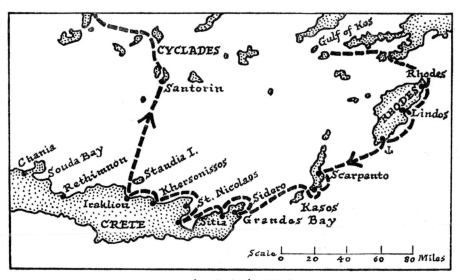

Suggested cruise in the S.E. Aegean

Spinalonga. A shallow lagoon formed by an island, well sheltered from the sea. The approach can be dangerous during the Meltemi on account of violent squalls from the high land close above.

> **Approach and Anchorage.** Chart 2536 B gives sufficient information. Pass north of Leper's Island and if proceeding to the top of the shallow fjord keep one third over from the eastern shore. There is also anchorage off the place styled 'Turkish cemetery' on chart 2850 in 2½ fathoms. Excellent holding, but violent gusts come down the mountain during the Meltemi, and in this case a sailing yacht of moderate draft is strongly advised to anchor at the top of the fjord.
>
> **Port Facilities.** At Elunta village limited provisions can be obtained and there is a bus service to St Nikolo.

Spinalonga was used by Imperial Airways during the thirties for seaplanes routed to Egypt and India. There is now a small hamlet at 'Turkish cemetery' with a daily bus service to St Nikolo. On the island of Spinalonga (Leper's Island) the old Venetian and Turkish buildings remain, but the island is uninhabited.

Khersonissos Bay, though rather open is reasonably well sheltered from the Meltemi.

> **Approach and Anchorage.** The anchorage is easy to find by day, but it would not be possible at night. There is plenty of swinging room in 2½ fathoms on firm sand well sheltered from N.N.W., but a swell rolls in. A yacht may lie comfortably with a kedge to hold her bows on to the swell.
>
> The ancient harbour at Khersonissos is still there, but silted, and is only used by small boats. A poor village of five hundred people, with an adjoining brick factory, lies south of the old port.
>
> There is only a modest taverna in the village, and no shops.

> *—the shore with mournful prospects, crown'd;*
> *The rampart torn with many a fatal wound*
> *The ruin'd bulwark tottering o'er the strand;*
> *Bewail the stroke of War's tremendous hand.*
> FALCONER, sailor-poet (at that time second mate in one of the British Levant Co. ships, 100 years after the great Siege of Candia).

Heraklion or **Iraklion.** A well-sheltered steamer port with an unattractive town, but a useful centre for visiting Knossos.

> **Approach and Berth.** Chart 2536 B is quite sufficient—there being no difficulty day or night. A yacht should proceed into the Venetian basin. Opposite the Venetian fortress turn

to port and berth stern to eastern mole, bows W.N.W. in 2 fathoms. Mud bottom. Here it is well sheltered; only a limited surge may be expected with northerly gales. The castle provides excellent shelter from a strong Meltemi.

Officials. A Port of Entry with Customs, Health, Immigration and Harbour authorities close by, where weather forecasts may also be obtained.

Port Facilities. There are now some first-class hotels, and half a dozen more modest ones; also many small restaurants in the centre of the town where, in a street of their own, good food can be served at a reasonable price. Provisions can be bought at the market at the top of the main street. Ice may be obtained at a store by the Museum Square (the road running eastward from the Port). Good water is available by hose from the steamer quay by prior arrangement with the Harbour-master.

General. Air communication with Athens several times a day; Piraeus steamers call every day during the summer.

Known until recent years by its Venetian name of Candia, the town has a population of fifty-five thousand. It is a useful centre for making excursions into the island. Taxis may be hired and most drivers know the country well. The Tourist Police will answer any queries regarding excursions or tourist amenities and will arrange a guide for Knossos where neither guides nor guide-books are available. Both Knossos, Phaestos and Ayia Triada should be visited, and certainly the museum in Heraklion, one of the most famous in the world.

Standia (also called Dia), an off-lying island, is 6 miles to the N.N.E. It is hilly and barren. Of the two coves, that lying to the N.E. affords useful anchorage in northerly winds. It is sometimes used by fishermen.

Rethimnon, Chart 1658, is claimed to be a well-sheltered port with a small characteristically Turkish town adjoining. Though little used by yachts, fuel, water and provisions are readily available. Only approachable if shallow draft.

Souda Bay, Chart 1658, provides the best shelter in Crete and for many years was used by large fleets as a base for exercises: it was used in World War II for the evacuation of British Forces from Greece. Tall mountains rise steeply either side of the bay, and during strong winds gusts sometimes sweep down the slopes into the bay.

A small naval depot lies at the head of the bay behind a protecting mole, and this is sometimes visited by minor vessels of the Greek Navy. The adjoining village has few amenities, but the town of Chania is barely three miles distant. Souda Bay has been mentioned as a good laying-up port, and permission to use its facilities should be applied for to the Greek Navy.

The Piraeus steamer calls every day.

Chania (hitherto spelt Khania and more recently Hania), though smaller than Heraklion is the capital of Crete, with a population of forty thousand people.

Its small harbour was built by the Venetians, and though picturesque is a poor little place for a yacht.

> **Approach and Berth.** Chart 1658. During strong northerly winds entry should not be attempted, and under moderate conditions the molehead should be given a generous offing. The quay by the galley sheds (now warehouses) is the best place to berth, though this is very inadequate. The depths here are about 2 fathoms, but the bottom is hard smooth rock on which no anchor will bite sufficiently to hold off a yacht during adverse conditions. A swell enters the port during fresh onshore winds.
>
> **Officials.** Though no steamer calls, this is a Port of Entry, with the usual organization of officials.
>
> **Port Facilities.** There is a number of restaurants around the quay and plenty of shops nearby. The town is pleasant and unspoilt by tourists; a motor road now connects it with Heraklion and other places on the north coast.
>
> **Excursions.** By bus to the monastery of Ayia Triada, thence on foot to Goberneto and the cave.

Gramvoussa (formerly Grabousa) is an isolated and insecure anchorage beneath steep cliffs on the N.W. of Crete. Sheltered by an island of this name, it has been seldom used since the last century when British frigates stamped out piracy. In the two years prior to the subjugation of Grabousa, a total of 155 ships were plundered and their cargoes disposed of at Grabousa. Of these 28 wore the English flag.

With northerly winds there is good shelter, but should the wind shift to W. or S.W. one should clear out.

The CYCLADES
(KIKLADHES)

7

The Cyclades

According to *Sailing Directions* there are nineteen islands encircling Delos, once a holy city and centre of the Confederation. Some of these islands are small or unimportant, and nearly all are largely barren, for they lack water and vegetation, and produce little in excess of their actual needs. In ancient Greek days, the best of the marble used in statuary and architecture was hewn in some of these islands and minerals also were obtained; today there is a small export of cattle, honey, oil, olives and wine.

At the present time the standard of living is low, and the life-line of these islanders is the bi-weekly steamer to Piraeus as well as the ubiquitous caique which plies among the islands. Though poor, they are a friendly people with a surprising poise and dignity which impresses many a newly-arrived stranger.

Though these islands have a common pattern, the character of each differs from that of its neighbour, the heterogeneous styles in architecture betraying the variety of their previous rulers. The houses are mostly in the form of a cube, painted a dazzling white, with a flat roof, in contrast to the eastern islands of, say, Samos, Chios, and parts of Mytilene, whose villages are in the Turkish style with red tile roofs and projecting balconies. In Santorin and Naxos there is some Venetian influence.

The principal town, or Chora, is usually known by the same name as the island. The Chora was often in a high position on a hill, originally built (for defence against pirates) with the stronger outer walls of the houses side by side and without openings. Sometimes the houses were grouped closely together outside the castle, which in case of attack became a refuge for the inhabitants as at Astipalea*. Very occasionally the village of the port has also been the capital, and examples of this kind are Mykonos and Paros; but nearly always the ever-latent fear of piracy drove the people of these Aegean islands to the safer alternative of establishing their Chora inland. To augment this natural form of self-preservation, the land-owners sometimes built fortified towers, and though these have largely disappeared, traces of them could be found recently in

* In the Dodecanese.

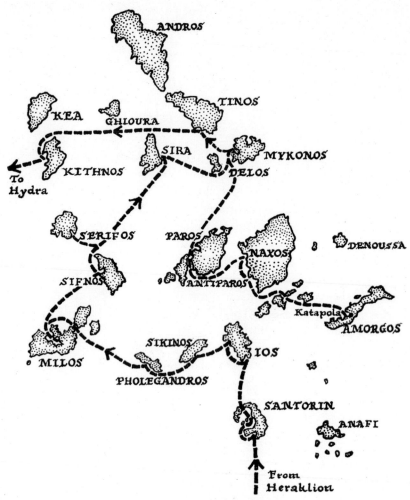

Suggested cruise in the Cyclades

Astipalea, Andros, Chios, Kithnos, Skiathos, Skopelos and Amorgos.

Only a strong Navy could suppress piracy and it was not until a final effort was made by British frigates in the early part of the nineteenth century that these islanders, after many centuries of fear and suffering, at last felt their safety assured. This had its influence on the ports, for from then onward the life of the port began to overshadow that of the inland Chora.

The great excitement in the port nowadays is the arrival of the Piraeus steamer, whose approach is heralded well in advance by the port authority. People appear from nowhere and immediately assemble, closely-packed, on the quay, the travellers encumbered with boxes, suitcases, baskets, children and chickens. This event may take place at any time during the day or night, and as everyone knows the steamer will not wait, they jostle along, unable to suppress their excitement at the prospect of a glimpse of the outside world. At some of the better-developed islands there are berthing-quays where the steamer may lie snugly alongside; but at many places she anchors outside the harbour and the intending passengers must pile into rowboats which, when closely packed, are then rowed off to the waiting ship. Very often the state of the sea at the anchorage is far from smooth and everyone gets splashed by the spray. Once alongside the steamer they must scramble up a narrow rickety accommodation ladder; old and young, children, baggage, and the chickens constantly urged to hurry by the sailors. Few of these people can afford any sheltered accommodation on board and so at night they huddle together travelling as deck passengers which, during the cold winter weather, must be the height of discomfort.

The boats return with the incoming passengers who have disembarked from the steamer. For them the discomfort of the voyage is over; sea-sickness forgotten, as well as the indignity of being bundled down ladders into a plunging boat—this is all in the past, and the whole family has turned up on the quay to welcome them back from Athens. If this should be in the day-time, then they pause at the taverna—for the men a glass of ouzo with *mezes* (cheese, olives, gherkins) or *dolmades* (meat and rice in vine leaves) or *garides* (prawns),— the women may prefer *baklava*, the children *loukoumi* (Turkish Delight) from Syra or Andros. All will like fruit. Then there is coffee, served in the Turkish manner with a glass of cold water.

Among the people living in the Chora, one invariably comes upon the 'American' type. He is generally to be recognized by the broad-brimmed hat, gold teeth and a massive gold ring. The few offensive ones will call out 'Hey Johnny' to the passing Englishman or American; but others of a quieter nature politely offer to interpret and to help with the shopping. In every island a number of the young men migrate to America, Canada and Australia. A surprisingly large proportion return to their native island in their old age, in order to spend the last years of their lives among the quiet, simple surroundings of their boyhood. For the visitor they are often a great help in elucidating unknown facts about the people and the place, and thus contribute to the understanding of the local people.

Amorgos, a long narrow island with tall mountains and precipitous cliffs, is primitive and quite unspoilt. The small hamlet of the port lines the quayside at the head of Katapola Bay:

Approach and Berth. Chart 1866 shows sufficient detail. If approaching from southward the monastery of Khozoviotissa stands out in white many miles away. When in the vicinity of the Katapola Bay one should head for the S.W. corner.

Proceed nearly to the head of the bay where there is a sandy beach and a smaller bridge. After passing a point where the quay diverges towards the S.W., 'let go' in about 7 fathoms on a mud bottom which rises steeply. The stern may then be hauled in to the quay where there is 10 feet depth and normally very clear water.

The lee formed by the divergence of the quay is most effective, especially with a west wind when a warp should be run out to hold up a vessel's bow. It is claimed that even a strong westerly does not endanger a vessel in this berth.

Port Facilities. There is a water tap only 10 yards from the above berth and along the quay-side are some small shops where fresh provisions may be bought—local oranges and vegetables are good. There is a bar, and in summer a small restaurant.

Petrol may be bought from drums. A Jeep runs up the hill to the Chora, leaving daily at 7 a.m. By night the only lighting is by oil lamps.

The Piraeus steamer calls.

Katapola is quite unspoilt and so is the Chora—a typical Cycladic village of white houses clustered round the old Castro on the mountain spur. As one approaches a number of very small churches with barrel roofs are to be seen near the roadside.

The visit to Khozoviotissa Monastery—half-an-hour's walk along a mule track from the Chora—is the main object of a call here. This small twelfth-century monastery partly built into a cavern is supported by its massive white buttresses projecting upon a vertical cliff face. Far below, the waves of the blue Aegean can be seen beating against the rocks.

When the traveller, Bent, came here in the latter part of the last century he had to enter by a drawbridge 'with fortifications against pirates'. He described the whole setting as being 'truly awful'. Unoccupied for many years, during which period many of its treasures were removed elsewhere, the monastery is now inhabited by four monks.

The island of Amorgos had a population of nearly four thousand in 1956; it is slowly declining, many of the young men leaving to seek a more profitable living elsewhere.

Andros, one of the largest and most northerly of the Cyclades, has a mountain ridge with peaks rising to over 3,000 feet. Though from the coast the rising slopes appear barren, the small town and villages support a population of seventeen thousand. The main life is in the two harbours:

(*a*) **Port Gavrion** is spacious, well sheltered, with a pleasant village on the water-front.

Approach and Anchorage. Chart 1833 (plan). There is no difficulty making up for the harbour entrance though caution is necessary at night to avoid the Vovi shoal. In seeking shelter during the Meltemi strong gusts are experienced when beating into the harbour.

Let go, as convenient off, the village in 3 fathoms. At the seaward end of the quay there is sufficient depths for a small yacht to lie stern to with anchor north or south.

Facilities. Limited fresh supplies are obtainable. There are one or two bars and a modest restaurant.

(*b*) **Port Kastro** has now become more important on account of the main village adjoining. The harbour with its short breakwater affords only limited protection, and though the holding is good the port is quite untenable in strong N.E. winds.

Andros from seaward is remarkable for the unusual stone walls, composed of thin slabs standing on edge, which mark the boundaries of the apparently neglected properties.

Anti-Paros is a dull island with the village of Kastro and a famous grotto. Its interest for a yacht lies mainly in the 14-foot passage and the harbour of Despotico.

Approach to the 14-foot passage is shown on Chart 1832, described as Anti-Paros Strait or 'Stenon Parou' in *Sailing Directions*. The view from southward of the giant rocks on the north side of the passage is impressive.

Anchorage. The harbour of Despotico is frequented by caiques and has the reputation of being a good all-weather port. It has convenient depths and good holding. Formerly, in the sixteenth and seventeenth centuries, it was the laying-up port for all the pirate vessels, including Genoese, French and Maltese galleys.

The grotto, which lies $1\frac{1}{2}$ miles from the sea and four from the village, is now electrically lit. It is recorded that in 1673 the French ambassador to the Porte came here with 500 followers, and celebrated the Christmas Mass. He afterwards removed several of the statues which had been hidden in the grotto and took them to Paris: some of them may be seen in the Louvre today.

Delos. The extensive ruins of Delos, former head of the Delian Confederation are of great interest. Barren, low-lying and uninhabited (except for the museum caretakers) the island is visited daily by hundreds of tourists. They come from Piraeus by steamer to Mykonos and thence by caique to Delos; having seen the ruins they are ferried back in the afternoon to their steamers. Facilities and conditions for a yacht at Delos are poor.

Anchorage. Chart 1815. Anchorage in the main channel is inadvisable on account of the foul nature of the bottom. A yacht drawing not more than 7 feet may berth by the existing built-up mole in the ancient port. (During the Meltemi, the north wind whistles through the

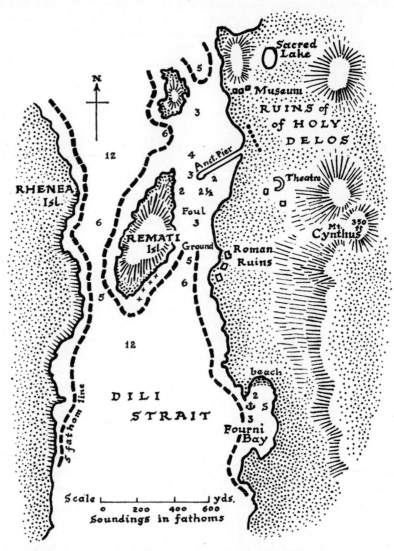

Delos. Fourni Bay, though very small, is the most comfortable anchorage, especially during Meltemi conditions, when the north wind often blows with gale strength. The pier, now built up, provides a possible berth for small vessels on the south side at the main landing

Dili Strait with great strength all day.) It is safer and quite comfortable to anchor in the small bay of Fourni, close under the north point in 3 fathoms. A landing may be made by dinghy at the sandy beach close by.

By the main site of the ruined temples is the museum and a small hostel with a shop selling local handicrafts. A guide may be hired if desired. All around are drums of columns, plinths of broken colonnades and foundations of vanished temples all broken off at a low level; only the terrace of lions in white Naxion marble stands out, forming an impressive approach to the temple as one walks up from the port. Appearing considerably less robust than lions of today, their lean bodies may perhaps have been the sculptor's licence in those early days of the seventh century B.C. Close by is the dried-up sacred lake and the bases of columns which once formed the Temple of Apollo.

Winding up the hillside is a narrow cobbled street leading to the theatre—on either side are the stone walls of once elegant houses with little niches to take the lanterns which lit the street.

The restored private houses are in much better state than the remains of the temples themselves; there are terra cotta stoves, marble tables, and well-heads, some inner courtyards with colonnaded verandahs, portions of paintings and stuccos (resembling those at Pompeii) and some remarkably complete and interesting mosaic pavements.

The ruins seen today are largely relics of the Confederation days and of the early Roman period.

Brief History. The early legends tell of Delos rising from the sea and becoming the refuge of the pregnant Latona and so the birth-place of Apollo and Artemis. As a holy shrine it was respected in later years by some of its conquerors, and there is a story of Polycrates of Samos securing the Holy Island to its neighbour Rhenea with a chain. In the fifth century, not only was the population removed, but the dead were disinterred and reburied in Rhenea.

After the Persian invasion, the Cyclades Islands formed a confederation, with Delos as their head, to provide mutual assistance, so that funds might be collected and conveyed to Athens for the purpose of building warships to be available for defence in the event of another invasion from the east. The funds were kept in the Delian Treasury and then sent to Athens as a contribution towards the construction of the navy. In 424 B.C., under pretext of safety, this treasury was transferred to Athens and subsequently much of the money was taken for building the Acropolis.

In the early Roman era this island was made into a free port, and though destroyed later by Mithryades, it became, according to Strabo, a great centre of commerce, 'thousands of slaves changing masters in a day'; they were provided by pirates to satisfy the needs of Rome, and both the kings of Egypt and of Syria co-operated in this trade.

In the later centuries it was plundered many times and writers have referred to its statues being broken up and made into lime. From the seventeenth century onwards one may read of ships visiting the island partly for the purpose of exercising the crew and also for collecting and bringing off pieces of marble to take home as presents.

Randolf, writing in 1687, stated 'The ruins are carried away by all ships who come to anchor there, so as part are in England, France, Holland, but mostly Venice'. Those making the grand tour a century later, would, as a matter of course, help themselves to what they could remove from Holy Delos—some of its finer sculptures have reached England during this period.

French archaeologists claim to have excavated a slipway longer than any found in Piraeus. Perhaps this discovery may lend support to an observation by Pausanias—'I have yet to hear that any man has built a larger vessel than the one at Delos which is banked for 9 banks of oars'.

A stone stairway ascends to the top of Mount Cynthus, and from here one has the clearest impression of the island. Close beneath lies the ancient port, the holy lake, the temple foundations and dwellings. In the cool of the evening, when the north wind abates, a peaceful quiet descends upon the island and one can feel the ruins reflecting something of their strange eventful history. Most impressive of all is to land in the evening when the moon is full; shining brilliantly on the white marble lions, they appear quite ghostlike in an eerie stillness broken only by the occasional bark from a shepherd's dog.

> *Such is the aspect of this shore;*
> *'Tis Greece, but living Greece no more.*
> *So coldly sweet, so deadly fair,*
> *We start, for soul is wanting there.*
>
> BYRON

Ios is a barren, though inviting island of gentle slopes, having three or four sheltered inlets as well as the attractive Ios Bay close to the island's capital.

Approach. Chart 2753. Ios Bay can be entered by night as well as by day. The other anchorages by day only.

In Ios Bay (see plan) there is good holding and shelter 150 yards from landing quay in 4 fathoms. The other bays are more exposed to the Meltemi gusts from the mountains.

Port Facilities. At the port of Ios there are now a couple of tavernas, where ice is obtainable as well as a light meal. The small attractive town is 20 minutes' walk up the hill and here there are shops for limited fresh supplies. There is running tap water laid on in the street.

General. A few caiques call here and also, during summer, a number of yachts. The Piraeus steamer calls twice a week.

Known as 'Little Malta' to the Turks on account of the good shelter, this bay was used some two centuries ago for careening small British ships.

Though there is nothing of antiquity save the site of one of the many tombs of Homer, it is refreshing to look upon the lovely features of this little island.

A memorable occasion was in 1692 when his Majesty's hired ship, the 'Arcana', galley, sank as she was being careened. Mr Roberts* who had saved himself but lost all his possessions, describes how he was captured by Corsairs and made to work for them on board as Gunner for many months suffering great hardship. He writes 'twelve rogues . . . laid hold of me, and carrying me on board on the starboard side, when I no sooner ascended but came a fellow and clapped a chain on my leg, and no-one spoke to me one word'.

* 'Mr. Roberts' adventures among the Corsairs of the Levant 1699'

Anchorage on the South Coast. Manganari Bay in the south is another suitable anchorage but rather exposed to gusts of wind during Meltemi. There is nothing here of interest.

Kea, formerly spelt Zea, is a mountainous island supporting nearly four thousand people, but of little importance today. Its shape and contours are remarkable especially when seen from the air: the high central ridge (1,800 feet) with its deep cut barren valleys fall symmetrically away on either coast to oak forestation and the sea.

St Nikolao is the only good harbour. It was once of some importance as a coaling station for steamers plying between west European ports and the Black Sea. This spacious sheltered bay has two arms, the northern one, Vourkari Bay, providing much the best shelter and good anchorage in depths up to 7 fathoms. The southern arm, Livardhi Bay, has a small boat harbour often used by caiques when the swell is not too disturbing. Both bays have a small hamlet where limited supplies can be obtained. There is plenty of fresh water on the island. A road joins the two hamlets which are a mile apart. From Livardhi a road leads up the mountain to the main village of Kea, standing one thousand feet up, and about three miles distant. Three miles beyond Kea is a large rock-hewn lion in bas-relief cut on the face of a rock.

Temporary Anchorages are to be found round the coast of which Kavia Bay is suitable in the summer months. In its eastern cove are convenient depths off some little houses at the head of the bay where small fishing boats are often based.

Kithnos, formerly Thermia, an island of 2,500 people is of no particular interest, though it has a number of inlets suitable for summer anchorages.

(*a*) **Port Merika** is a sheltered inlet with a few small houses and is used as the port for Kithnos, the main village. Though the two coves northward of Merika provide better shelter, they have poor communication with Kithnos village.

Approach and Anchorage. Chart 1817. A flashing light was recently established on the water-front southward of a small stone pier projecting from the northern shore by some small houses. Here are depths of 3 fathoms on a bottom of mud, but the shore soon rises steeply towards the head of the bay. The holding here is good, but the shelter not adequate in strong N.W. winds.
Facilities. Supplies must be obtained from Kithnos village some 3 or 4 miles along the road leading inland. The Piraeus steamer calls three times a week.

(*b*) **Loutron,** an uninteresting anchorage with partial shelter, off a former 'Cure Resort', on the N.E. side of the island.

Approach and Anchorage. The white Hydro and small houses are visible some distance to seaward. The most convenient anchorage is in the S.E. creek where half-way along are depths of 3 fathoms on a sandy bottom (also some weed and small stones). There are one or two bollards for warps on the northern shore. Shelter is reasonably good.

Facilities. Limited provisions may be bought locally and there are one or two bars in the small hamlet. The Piraeus steamer calls once a week in the summer months. Kithnos village is 40 minutes' walk along a road.

Though hardly any visitors come to this place, the old thermal baths establishment, built for Greece's first King Otto, is still kept open.

An ore-tip and a mooring buoy in the exposed bay are relics of a mining concern no longer in operation.

Mykonos or Mikonos, a semi-barren island, lying close northward of Delos. Its port serves as a base when tourists arrive in the steamers from Piraeus, and are then ferried by the local caiques to Delos.

Anchorage. Chart 1833. Steamers anchor in the middle of the harbour, and yachts often berth among the caiques at the S.W. corner. A more sheltered and agreeable berth also suitable for bathing is off the north mole with bows S.E. The Meltemi can make the southern part of the harbour uncomfortable.

Facilities. Fresh provisions can be bought; there are one or two tavernas and two small modern hotels.

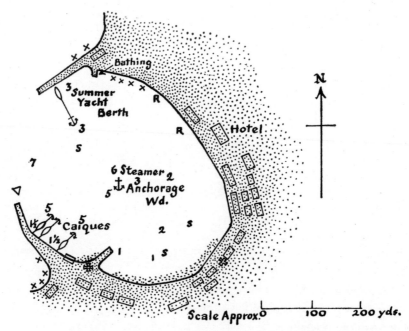

Mykonos: a rough survey by author. (*Soundings in fathoms*)

White houses line the crescent-shaped harbour with the small town rising on the slopes behind. Along the ridge above the slopes are the white-painted wind-mills which continue to grind the corn of the island.

Though the country is almost barren and without interest, yet the town is charming with its dazzling white houses—sometimes of two or three stories—with doors and shutters in green, and little churches with blue domes. The narrow winding streets are pleasant to wander through, having the occasional attraction of a small square, a Venetian well-head, or an outside stairway.

A local industry of cotton-weaving has grown up, and clothing, such as shirts, skirts and belts, is now attractively put on display for sale to tourists.

Milos, a volcanic island with mountains forming a circle round a huge bay, with its port of **Adamas.**

Approach and Berth. Chart 2051 makes pilotage easy, and lights having now been established on Lakida Pt and Bombarda, entry by night presents no difficulty. Two jetties not shown on the chart have now been built out extending southwards from the shore at Adamas. The westernmost is used by the mail steamer and small freighters which berth alongside. A yacht may berth at the extremity of the eastern pier in depths of 2 fathoms or anchor off. The bay being large would not afford much shelter to a small yacht in the event of a blow from the southern quadrant; but it is one of the best harbours among the islands for small steamers. The holding on the sandy bottom is good.

Port Facilities. The unattractive port of Adamas is of recent development; it has a few shops and a modest restaurant—limited fresh provisions are available. There is no tap-water, but a tank lorry may be obtained if given notice. Ice can be bought. The Piraeus steamer calls three times a week.

Half-an-hour's drive takes one to the Chora, attractively built upon the hill over Hellenic remains, with a Greek theatre,* and a Venetian castle on the summit. The village, which is interesting and still unspoilt, affords fine views over the surrounding fjords and nearby islands.

The island's population of nearly eleven thousand people is mostly occupied in mining sulphur, bensonite, barium. There are some villages connected by roads. The lower slopes of the mountains are largely covered with scrub, and there is some cultivation.

Earlier History. During the centuries of Turkish domination, the island enjoyed much prosperity, and so long as it paid tribute to the Pasha no force was ever used to prevent its harbour from being used as a great base for pirates. It was here they brought their prizes for disposal and consequently the port grew rich as a mercantile transhipment centre.

* It was within 200 yards of this theatre that the famous Venus—now in the Louvre—was found in 1820.

Naxos. This is the largest and most mountainous island of the Cyclades. 'La plus grande et la plus belle' says the *Guide Bleu*. Because of its agriculture and the activity in the harbour it gives the impression of having a brisk trade. The quayside is usually animated with café life, restaurants and tavernas, buses and taxis, steamers coming and going, and caiques loading and unloading. This island now supports a population of 18 thousand.

> **Approach and Berth.** Chart 1832. The harbour can be uncomfortable in N.W. blows, though an additional inner breakwater has recently improved the shelter. Under normal summer conditions, a yacht may anchor off the centre of the town in about 3 fathoms.
>
> **Port Facilities.** Most things may be bought at the shops on the quay. Taxis are available. Two or three restaurants are on the quay front. Petrol from a pump.
>
> The Piraeus steamer calls almost daily in summer.

What remains of the old Venetian town built on the side of the hill is interesting. Extending round the quay there is an old winding street crossed by arches; Venetian doorways, pediments and occasional coats of arms can be found.

There are one or two pleasant excursions to be made by car: perhaps the most interesting is to the colossal statue, possibly Apollo (34 feet tall), cut in marble near the northern end of the island.

In very early days Naxos was famous for its wine and it was here that Dionysos (Bacchus) is reputed to have found Ariadne (daughter of the Cretan King) after her desertion by Theseus. The Venetians made good use of the island early in the thirteenth century when Marco Sanudo, taking advantage of the decadence of the Byzantine empire, captured it. The descendants of this great adventurer, who set themselves up as Dukes of Naxos, ruled this island and others of the Cyclades for 350 years until overwhelmed by the Turks in 1566. The islands were not restored to Greece until after the liberation in 1832.

> **Other Anchorages Nearby.** (a) South of Kurupa Point is a sandy bay with excellent shelter and holding—an ideal temporary anchorage when working to windward against a freshening Meltemi.
>
> (b) North of Heraklia is a sandy bay (known as St Georgios) with convenient depths and excellent shelter from winds other than Meltemi. There is a small hamlet and a few fishing craft.
>
> The Piraeus steamer calls here once a week.

Paros, lying barely three miles across the Strait, is similar to Naxos, but half its size. The bare central massif with two prominent peaks is surrounded by attractive coastal plains. Of the two harbours, Paroikia on the N.W. adjoining the principal town makes an interesting port of call for a yacht. Naussa in the north, though described in *Sailing Directions* as 'One of the best ports in the

Cyclades' is more suitable for larger vessels and is unpleasantly open to the north.

(a) Paroikia

Anchorage. Chart 1832. *Sailing Directions* and plan provide the necessary data. Though open to west the local people claim that shelter is adequate. It should be noted that the pier-head

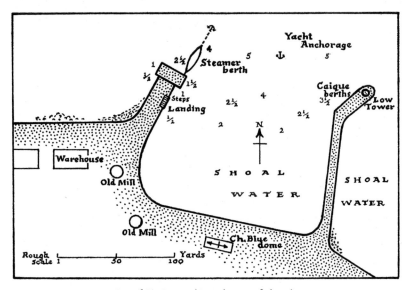

Paroikia, Paros. (*Soundings in fathoms*)

is kept clear for the Piraeus steamer which in summer calls daily, and the rest of the quay is used by local caiques. It is therefore advisable for a yacht to anchor off.

Port Facilities. Water can be obtained from a tap about 100 yards from the root of the pier. There is an ice factory close by. Petrol may be bought from drums at a depot 200 yards away by the village. There are limited fresh provisions, and two or three simple restaurant-bars; a modern hotel has recently been built in a commanding position just beyond the village.

The pleasant white village of Paroikia, extending along the sea front, is reminiscent of Naxos with some outside stairways and arcades. A number of Greek tourists come here in the summer.

The Church of Our Lady with a hundred Gates lies on the eastern side of the village and is the most curious and interesting in the Aegean. Parts of it are said to date from the time of Justinian; but it has been altered and extended during the years and is now really three churches in one. The early Byzantine columns and the triforium should be noted.

Wine, corn, and some marble are exported from Paroikia. Some attempt has been made to improve the roads and also to promote facilities for summer tourists.

In the whole island there are nearly 10,000 people; the country in spring is attractive with green valleys and partially wooded slopes. There are some pleasant walks.

The famous white marble of the ancient days was mostly quarried underground by Mt Marpessa, now passed on the road to Lykos, five kilometres out from Paroikia. After many centuries of disuse the quarries suddenly came into operation again in 1844 when this marble was required for the tomb of Napoleon.

(b) **Naussa.** This place used to be severely afflicted with malaria. Once a main base for the Russian fleet under Alexis Orloff after 1770, it had large shore installations; but after a few years the base had to be hurriedly abandoned on account of the declining state of health among the sailors.

> **Anchorage.** Chart 1832 shows an excellent plan and indicates the anchorages suitable for a yacht in the N.W. and N.E. corners of this large bay. Though protected from sea and wind, there is the reflection of a swell during the Meltemi.

Santorin or **Thira.** Appearing in the distance as a peakless cone, it is, in fact, an ancient volcano forming a circular island which has been split in two by a tremendous eruption; possibly the same great upheaval, with attendant earthquakes and tidal waves, that some consider to have destroyed the Minoan palaces of Crete in Mycenean times. There has been a number of severe eruptions since those days, one alluded to by Strabo in the second century B.C. when 'flames rushed forth from the sea for a space of four days, causing the whole of it to boil and be on fire'.

Entering the wide, sheltered strait among the islands, a broad ribbon of white houses appears on the skyline above the sheer dark brown cliffs. This is Thira, the capital.

To the southward is the lava islet of Nea Caemene where caiques are often to be seen moored to the rocks in the sulphurous water above the little crater which still spews out its sulphur fumes through the sea bed beneath. Taking advantage of this natural benefit provided gratuitously by the sea bed, these vessels remain here for a day or two, after which their bottoms are foul no longer.

> **Berth.** Chart 2043. The small quay beneath the main village of Thira is easily distinguished by day. Though there are depths of 6 to 10 feet, the sea bed falls away very steeply. It is best to hold a yacht off the quay with a kedge anchor and long length of warp. There is a mooring buoy for steamers; in event of a swell or unsettled conditions it is advisable during the summer

months to proceed southwards and anchor in convenient depths under the lee of the southern shores of the island where both shelter and holding are good.

Facilities. Nothing is available at the quay, but normal fresh provisions can be bought in Thira and brought down by mule. These beasts are in good supply and the muleteers make a lucrative trade carrying tourists up and down between the landing and Thira.

⚓ *Safest Summer anchorages*

Santorin

The mule-track zigzags up the 700-foot precipitous slope. The sides of the cliff, once the interior of the crater, are sometimes ash-red and even black; often corrugated as if with pillars, interspersed here and there is a troglodyte dwelling.

The long narrow town of Thira clings to the top of the ridge. Its two streets lined with white houses and often spanned by arches are attractive. There is a cathedral and a Greek Orthodox Church, and the peal of bells is sometimes to be heard.

The view from the top is magnificent, for one appears to be standing almost directly above the quay with probably one or two yachts and caiques moored beneath. Across the deep blue water are the steep brown cliffs forming the opposite side of this one-time crater. The landward aspect reveals a plateau with vineyards; beyond are two other villages, and a monastery near the mountain peak, and in the distance other islands of the archipelago. This high plateau is agreeably peaceful after the disturbing impression made by the nether regions of the port.

One of Santorin's difficulties is shortage of water. Though rainwater is collected and run into the numerous cisterns at Thira, supplies are insufficient, and during the summer months a tanker from Piraeus must sometimes augment them.

The tourist trade contributes considerably to the resources of this island. In addition, there is an export of pumice and wine. These trades altogether support a population of 15 thousand.

Serifos, a hilly island with two large bays in the south, affording good anchorage in the summer months:

(*a*) **Livardhi Bay** with the Chora standing on the hill above is the more interesting place to anchor.

> **Approach and Anchorage.** Charts 1639 and 1833 (plan). Anchorage can be entered by day or night. The white village above stands out against the background and can be seen some miles distant. Caiques normally berth at the quay with a short pier. It is sometimes convenient for a yacht to berth stern to this pier, bows N.E., or alternatively to anchor in 3 fathoms in the N.W. corner of the bay. Here one is well sheltered, even in southerly winds.
>
> **Facilities.** There is nothing much to be had in the port, except ice; but little over half an hour's walk by a mule track leads to the Chora where fresh provisions can be bought.

(*b*) **Koutala Bay,** which is spacious and similar to Livardhi, has mooring buoys and iron-ore tips.

> **Approach and Anchorage.** Charts 1639 and 1833. The approach is easy by day, but mooring buoys might be a danger at night, especially in the N.W. corner of the bay. A suitable place to anchor is in the N.E. corner in depths of 2 to 3 fathoms.

Today the iron-ore workings can be seen on the hillside, and occasionally a small shipment is made. It was worked by the Romans and continued throughout the Middle Ages and so a small population has been maintained continuously. When the Venetian conquerors came they built a small fortress on one of the heights; but their navigators complained of their 'compass needles being disturbed by the iron ore'.

The island appears to be rather poor today; during its early Greek days the expression for an old maid was 'an old woman of Serifos'.

Sifnos (Siphnos), one of the less important islands, has some attractive sheltered bays and the unspoilt village of Apollonia standing on the hill in the centre.

(*a*) **Kamares,** the main port of Sifnos, lies in a pleasant bay in bare hilly surroundings.

Approach and Anchorage. Chart 1833 (plan). In addition to the charted green light, there is a red light on the end of the short harbour mole. Anchor in 2½ fathoms 70 yards N.W. of the mole on a sandy bottom. Though open only to west, this bay affords poor shelter in the Meltemi, and Vathy is infinitely better.

Facilities. Excellent water may be obtained from a hand pump at a spring at the eastern end of the village. There are tavernas and stores for limited fresh provisions. A bus runs frequently to Apollonia (the Chora) on the hill—20 minutes' drive.

The Piraeus steamer calls three times a week in summer. Above the port in Kamares bay a number of modern villas have been built belonging to Greeks living in Egypt who spend their holidays here.

Other anchorages on Sifnos are:

(*b*) **Port Vathy,** close southward of Kamares—a sandy bay, having nearly all-round shelter. The best anchorage is in the N.E. corner. The few inhabitants are mostly occupied with pottery.

(*c*) **Pharos,** in the south—an attractive sheltered inlet with a few houses and a road leading to Apollonia.

The island, which is far more green on the S.E. part, has a population of three thousand, mostly employed in growing olives and in making pottery. Both these products are exported by caique to other islands and to the Piraeus.

Apollonia, the former Kastro, was built by the Venetian Corogne family in the fifteenth century. Still unspoilt in 1960, it was about to have a cinema and modern hotel.

There are a few small villages on the island, now connected by roads.

Though of little importance today, in ancient times Sifnos was rich on account of its gold mines, and witness of this period is the marble treasury still to be seen nearly intact at Delphi.

Sira or **Syra,** capital of the Cyclades, has a town of more than twenty thousand people; the commercial activity in its spacious port, which made the island so important in the last century, is not so evident today.

The two main villages, the catholic Ano-Syra and the orthodox Hermoupolis are each perched on a hill beyond the harbour, their white houses reaching down to the port. Here is the small town with an impressive eighteenth-century square complete with public buildings and a small opera house—the most striking 'city centre' of the Aegean and quite un-Greek in appearance. Though there is no marked activity here today, the presence of a floating dock, some quays busy with loading and unloading caiques and small steamers, as well as some large vessels laid up, all tend to suggest a revival of commerce.

Approach and Berth. Chart 1639, and plan on 1833 show the entrance quite clearly. A yacht should proceed to the farthest quay, berthing 'stern to' and bows towards the entrance. This berth is among the caiques and is not a salubrious corner of the harbour; but the main quay is often occupied with commercial vessels. The harbour is well sheltered, though not clean.

Facilities. Most things can be obtained close by on the quayside. Water is difficult to obtain and can only be bought expensively from a tank-cart. There is a number of tavernas. It is possible for a yacht to slip on a skid cradle at the shipyard. The Piraeus steamer calls three times a week. In the summer a bus runs to Krasi Bay where there is a bathing beach.

Officials. A Port of Entry; there is the usual quota of officials.

The island has become best known to tourists for its manufacture of 'loukoumi' (Turkish Delight).

Historical Note. The British interest in Syra began after the founding of the Levant company in the reign of Queen Elizabeth, but its real prosperity was during the last century in the early days of steam.

After gaining her freedom from the Turks together with the rest of Greece in 1829, Syra found herself in a fortunate situation. Her commodious port lay in a strategic position on the trade route between the Black Sea, Levant and western ports. In those days steamers could proceed only limited distances without bunkering, and Syra's geographical position was in the precise locality to suit most routes. Thus the packet service, Egypt-Constantinople, Austro-Lloyd from Piraeus, Trieste and Brindisi, and the French Messageries ships, Bibby Line etc., all called here for bunkering; it became in consequence a market for British coal. With its growing commercial importance consular representation was established; in addition to the British Consul there were nine consulates of other nations, and a British church and chaplain.

Syra has never been devastated by foreign invaders nor persecuted by the Turks as has happened to other islands. It was fortunate in having had a Capuchin mission which for centuries had the protection of France, and the Turks never molested them. It seems that this happy state of security attracted refugees who had fled from other islands, and thus at the time of the boom in shipping the man-power was available to help develop the resources of the port.

At the beginning of this century when oil began to take the place of coal, the importance of Syra declined and today there seems only limited activity in the port, mostly confined to repair work.

Here, as in so many of these islands, the interest is entirely in the port, for the country is unwelcoming. The bleak mountains of Syra with their lower slopes now so barren and tree-less, bear no resemblance to their description nearly three thousand years ago by Homer:

> 'Of soil divine,
> a good land teeming with fertility,
> Rich with green pastures, feeding flocks and kine
> a fair land with streams, a land of corn and wine.'
>
> ODYSSEY XV

Tinos. The island is remarkable today as being the 'Lourdes of Greece.'

This well-sheltered port with an interesting town in mountainous surround-ings should be visited.

Since 1822, when the miraculous icon of the Panagia was discovered, pilgrims from Greece have flocked to Tinos every year to attend the great feast of Our

A votive offering in Tinos church (see p. 160)

Lady. Tinos has thus become a place of pilgrimage and the local inhabitants have prospered as a result. They continue to do so today.

Approach and Berth. Chart 1833 (plan). Secure stern to the northern quay with anchor towards entrance. (Eastwards of the second bollard from the west it has been dredged.) Though a new loading quay has now been built out to the southward from the main quay, it is often overcrowded with caiques working their cargoes.

Facilities. Water, said to be the purest in Greece, is supplied by a tap close by. There are plenty of provisions available. There is one small hotel and one or two restaurants. Local wine is pleasant. There are now two petrol-filling stations on the quay. The local weaving industry has some good examples in a shop up the hill.

The harbour is large and the quays are often animated with people at the bars and tavernas which line the water-front. There is usually a number of brightly-painted caiques loading and unloading their cargoes. This busy scene makes a contrast to the more restful atmosphere usually associated with the Cyclades.

Mail boats from Piraeus berth with a complicated manœuvre alongside the modern quay on the arm of the breakwater.

There are many mountain villages dotted around the island whose valleys have spring water at heights of 1,000 feet or more. In recent years farmers have taken up the grazing of Jersey herds, cattle being sometimes shipped from Tinos to Piraeus, tightly packed in the holds of small caiques.

From the quay, walking towards the hill, one soon approaches the large white Orthodox Church. Although of no architectural merit, the forecourt is attractive, as well as the courtyard of the convent whose glaring white walls are softened by the shadows of the dark cypresses.

Inside the church is the icon itself with typical Byzantine silverwork almost covering the painting of 'the great and gracious Lady'. Pilgrims are often wheeled in and the priests may be seen reciting their supplications, at the same time treating the pilgrims in no gentle manner as they twist them about, apparently to draw the Virgin's attention to that part of their anatomy they are beseeching her to cure. Hung from the roof of the church are many models, often in silver—the votive offerings given by those who have been saved from a violent death by the intervention of the Virgin. Perhaps one of the more curious is that of a caique which had been holed and was about to sink, but was saved by the timely arrival of a benign fish, which swam into the hole and so sealed it from the inrushing water. The hull, the sails and even the fish are skilfully and realistically worked in silver.

In the little crypt are two chapels, one marking the site of the discovery of the icon, and the other a memorial to the dead sailors of the Greek cruiser *Elli*. On 15 August 1940, when Greece was at peace with all nations, their cruiser *Elli* had been sent to attend the usual celebrations of Our Lady of Tinos, and lay at anchor outside the port. She had dressed ship in honour of the occasion and many of her ship's company were ashore. An Italian submarine operating under orders from Rome fired a torpedo, sinking her and many of the crew—an outrage the Greeks cannot easily forget.

The 'Dry Islands'. Both Sikinos and Folegandros are mountainous, barren and steep-to. They are very little visited, though both have open sandy bays and in summer they afford comfortable anchorage.

Sikinos

Anchorage. There is 2 fathoms close in and room to swing; the bottom is fine sand. A landing quay is on the western side of the small bay. The Meltemi produces a few strong gusts: it is entirely open to south.

Facilities. A small taverna and one or two small houses are on the quay, and there is a freshwater well 200 yards inland. Provisions must be obtained from the main village on the hill.

The Chora lies on the mountain ridge on the opposite side of the island—a village of 700 people. It is less than an hour's walk along an easy mule road and is worth the effort. The Orthodox church—Episcopi—is another hour onward; this was built round the former temple of Apollo whose Ionic columns still stand.

The population in 1960 was 800, nearly all of whom live in the one village. They are largely employed on cultivating the terraced vineyards and corn fields which cannot be seen from seaward.

Folegandros has no port, but a weekly steamer calls, anchoring off the main village.

Anchorages. (a) Karavostasi, with the island village adjoining, may be approached with aid of Chart 1832. A stony road leads up to the Chora.

(b) Vathy Bay has convenient depths on a sandy bottom; but being rather open a swell creeps round the bay during northerly winds.

The island, with a population of only 500 people, offers nothing of particular interest, though a walk to the Chora is rewarding. The coastline is remarkable for its tall steep-to cliffs. Though cultivation cannot be seen from the sea, a number of terraces in the valleys leading up to the Chora are still farmed.

The remaining three islands of the Cyclades are seldom visited:

Anafi (Anaphi) is a group of rather flat and largely barren islands with very few inhabitants living in the village on the south of the main island. Here is an open anchorage, but there is no harbour. Occasionally the island is overrun by a plague of partridges which cause havoc among the sparsely cultivated fields of the farmers.

Denoussa is little known, but the shelter it afforded to a German collier in August 1914 enabled the battle-cruiser *Goeben* to embark the necessary coal and so escape from the pursuing British forces. She reached Constantinople where her presence exerted considerable influence in forcing Turkey into the war as an ally of Germany.

Ghioura or **Ghiaros** is a small island sometimes still used, as it was by the Romans, as a penitentiary for prisoners. It was prohibited as a place of call.

Fair Greece! Sad relic of departed worth!
Immortal, though no more; though fallen, great!
BYRON

Appendix

LOCAL CRAFT

Until a few years ago the whole of the Aegean was remarkable for the numerous and distinctive types of sailing craft. They were without motors until the early twenties; but since then mechanical power has slowly displaced the need for the original sails.

Though some of the former hulls continue to be built today, they are to be seen only under power with 'steadying sails'—a poor apology for the handsome spread of canvas which once characterized them.

Aegean sailing craft. Caiques at Limnos during First World War, before motors came in.

The few old-timers among Greek sailors today are sometimes quite perplexed at being confronted with photographs of Aegean vessels of half a century ago and after some hesitation they will recognize the type of hull. Then, with still more doubt, they will specify the rig; although it sometimes happens that the particular rig originates from a district with which they are not familiar.

The 'Bratsera' or Aegean Lugger. This ubiquitous vessel with standing-lug main and balance-lug foresail can carry cargoes of 50 to 150 tons and more.

With an accentuated sheer and pronounced flare carried well aft, these boats

The ubiquitous lugger of the Aegean carries the trade of the islands. Nowadays only steadying sails are used, and the motor drives her along at 5 or 6 knots.

have a wide beam at deck level. A shallow keel, without ballast and little draft, makes them poor performers to windward. The low waist, protected against spray by a canvas screen laced to a light spar supported by gunwale-irons, is still a characteristic feature of all Aegean craft, except in the case of the large wine schooners.

The Turks, who formerly shared with the Greeks considerably more of the Aegean coast than they do today, also build these vessels. Though constructed largely by Greek shipwrights, the Turkish vessels have a still more accentuated sheer, giving them an almost crescent effect.

The origin of the hull and rig are difficult to determine, but there is good reason to believe that the rig is of Italian origin, probably from the north Adriatic. Except for a few in trade with the Ionian islands, these vessels are not seen outside the Aegean.

Construction. There are two types of hull: the 'Perama' and 'Trehanderi'. Similar in form, the Perama has a straight inclined stem, whereas the Trehanderi has a curved stem projecting with a sweep well above the gunwale. The Perama also has the stemhead forming a beak with athwartship bulkhead after the pre-Nelson style.

Built in considerable numbers at Piraeus, they are also built at Syra, Samos, Ikaria, Skiathos and other islands, all of pinewood from the forests of Samos, this timber being considered the most suitable for ship construction in the Aegean.

Planking-up starts from the covering board downwards and from the keel upwards at the same time, being fastened to doubled frames with galvanized nails. Instead of steaming the planks for an unwilling bend, they are soaked for a while in salt water. The gap where the planks meet sometimes requires a filling piece of most peculiar shape—quite horrifying to those unversed in Greek construction. In the more primitive island yards no drawings are used, but one or two standardized moulds may sometimes be seen put away on the walls of the builder's store. When asked how he builds to a particular shape or design, the reply is usually 'I build like my father taught me'.

When the construction is complete, caulking is applied here and there; after a coat of red-lead, the boat is then painted, nowadays in gay colours, sometimes a white hull with red gunwale, light blue or vermilion. The priest is asked to bless her and she is then launched before the admiring eyes of the owner's family and friends. The owner is often only part-owner; as much as half the money is sometimes lent by the banks.

The great majority of craft seen in the Aegean are the same Perama and Trehanderi hulls with Bratsera rig; but there are also other varieties.

Sacoulevi, where a Bermudian type mainsail sheeted to a boomkin is shortened by releasing the peak halyard, and brailing the sail to the mast. (Trehanderi hull.)

Spritsail rig, used by a number of small craft. This type of sail can be traced back to early Hellenic days. (Trehanderi hull.)

Latini rig (with the forefoot cut away to give place to a staysail). This rig was first known in the Mediterranean at the time of the Arab invasions. (Perama hull.)

Details of Perama beak, showing characteristic features of
pre-Nelson athwartship bulkhead and prominent bitts. This
vessel also has a cathead.

A deeply laden Perama accentuates the wide beam.

Index